Backroad Bicycling in
Western Massachusetts

Backroad Bicycling in Western Massachusetts

ANDI MARIE CANTELE

30 Rides in the
Berkshires,
Hampshire County,
the Mohawk Trail,
and the
Pioneer Valley

Backcountry Guides
Woodstock, Vermont

Library of Congress Cataloging-in-Publication Data
Cantele, Andi Marie, 1969–
    Backroad bicycling in western Massachusetts : 30 rides in the Berkshires, Hampshire County, the Mohawk Trail, and the Pioneer Valley.—1st ed.
        p. cm.
    ISBN 0-88150-559-5
    1. Bicycle touring—Massachusetts—Guidebooks. 2. Bicycle trails—Massachusetts—Guidebooks. 3. Massachusetts—Guidebooks. I. Title.
GV1045.5.M4 F87 2003
796.6'4'09744—dc21

                                        2002026032

Cover photo © Dennis Coello
Interior photographs by the author
Book design by Bodenweber Design
Composition by PerfecType, Nashville, TN
Maps by Moore Creative Design, © 2002 The Countryman Press

Published by Backcountry Guides, a division of The Countryman Press, P.O. Box 748, Woodstock, Vermont 05091

Distributed by W.W. Norton & Company, Inc., 500 Fifth Avenue, New York, NY 10110

Printed in the United States of America

10 9 8 7 6 5 4 3 2 1

For Brian

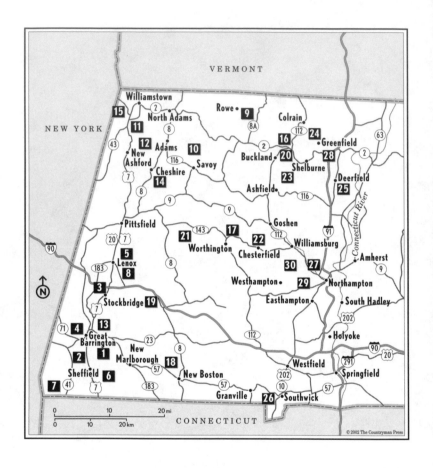

CONTENTS

ACKNOWLEDGMENTS This book was written with the support of many people whom I would like to thank and recognize.

There are many quality bike shops scattered across the region staffed by friendly, knowledgeable cyclists. Many contributed invaluable advice and route ideas, especially Paul Rinehart at The Spoke in Williamstown; Ken Gonsalves and Keith Dupuis at The Arcadian Shop in Lenox; Chris Ethier, Mark Bennett, and Jim Bonham at Bicycle World in Greenfield; Nathan Mealey at Northampton Bicycle in Northampton; Dave Drumm at Mean Wheels Bike Shop in Lenox; and Tom Martin at Ordinary Cycles in Pittsfield. I am grateful for their assistance and ideas.

Thanks also to Mike Ward of the Berkshire Cycling Association for his insight on cycling in western Massachusetts; Tim Baldwin, executive director of the Massachusetts Bicycle Coalition, for providing contacts in the bicycling community; Al Tiboni of Ride NoHo Inc. for his input on the Northampton rides; Tony Cantele for Ride #2: The Berkshires to the Twin Lakes; and Gus Orviston for helping me find the river roads.

Finally, special thanks goes to Ann Kraybill, Kermit Hummel, and Jennifer Thompson at Backcountry Guides for their advice and guidance; and to my family, once again, for their encouragement and support.

All of you helped make this book possible.

BACKROAD BICYCLE TOURS AT A GLANCE

RIDE	REGION	DISTANCE
1. Housatonic River Villages	Southern Berkshires	41.7 miles
2. The Berkshires to the Twin Lakes	Southern Berkshires	35.7 miles
3. Stockbridge	Southern Berkshires	28.8 miles
4. Great Barrington to New York	Southern Berkshires	27.4 miles
5. Lenox	Southern Berkshires	25.2 miles
6. Sheffield to Mill River	Southern Berkshires	19.0 miles
7. A Three-State Tour	Southern Berkshires	44.3 miles
8. Lee to Lenox	Southern Berkshires	18.9 miles
9. Deerfield River and Hoosac Range	Northern Berkshires	27.2 miles
10. The Northern Berkshires	Northern Berkshires	54.8 miles
11. Williamstown	Northern Berkshires	12.8 miles
12. Mount Greylock	Northern Berkshires	35.4 miles
13. The Berkshire Hills: A Two-Day Tour	Northern Berkshires	117.2 miles
14. Cheshire Reservoir	Northern Berkshires	9.5 miles

DIFFICULTY	BIKE	KIDS?	HIGHLIGHTS
Moderate to Strenuous	Road	No	Farms and antique homes along the Housatonic River
Moderate	Road	No	Berkshire County's oldest house
Moderate	Road	No	Historic New England villages
Strenuous	Hybrid	No	Rural countryside along the New York border
Moderate	Road	No	Tanglewood and the Stockbridge Bowl
Easy to Moderate	Hybrid	Yes	The hidden village of Mill River
Strenuous	Road	No	A scenic waterfall in the rugged Taconics
Easy to Moderate	Road	Yes	Grand 19th-century estates
Moderate to Strenuous	Hybrid	No	Hidden dirt roads above the Deerfield River
Strenuous	Road	No	Panoramic views from Western Summit
Easy	Hybrid	Yes	A classic New England college town
Strenuous	Road	No	The state's highest summit at 3,491 feet
Strenuous	Road	No	Hancock Shaker Village; October Mountain State Forest
Easy	Road	Yes	A pleasant loop around a reservoir

RIDE	REGION	DISTANCE
15. Across the Taconics: Williamstown to New York	Northern Berkshires	44.6 miles
16. Mohawk Trail Villages	Hampshire Hills	27.5 miles
17. The Hampshire Hills	Hampshire Hills	22.6 miles
18. New Boston to Otis	Hampshire Hills	22.3 miles
19. Beartown State Forest	Hampshire Hills	30.6 miles
20. River Roads: Shelburne Falls to Vermont	Hampshire Hills	54.8 miles
21. The Skyline Trail	Hampshire Hills	36.5 miles
22. Hills and Villages	Hampshire Hills	43.3 miles
23. Ashfield to Shelburne Falls	Hampshire Hills	22.8 miles
24. The Upper Pioneer Valley	Pioneer Valley	45.0 miles
25. Historic Deerfield	Pioneer Valley	20.0/35.5 miles
26. The Southwick Jog	Pioneer Valley	28.6 miles
27. The Connecticut River: Northampton to Sunderland	Pioneer Valley	23.8 miles
28. The Connecticut River: Greenfield to Sunderland	Pioneer Valley	26.3 miles
29. The Hamptons	Pioneer Valley	23.6 miles
30. Northampton to Chesterfield	Pioneer Valley	25.0 miles

DIFFICULTY	BIKE	KIDS?	HIGHLIGHTS
Strenuous	Road	No	A challenging route over the Taconic Range
Moderate	Road	No	A flower-filled bridge in an eclectic village
Strenuous	Road	No	The historic William Cullen Bryant Homestead
Moderate	Hybrid	No	Meandering dirt roads through quiet forest
Moderate to Strenuous	Road	No	Bear Mountain State Forest
Moderate to Strenuous	Road	No	Twisting river roads; rural Vermont villages
Strenuous	Road	No	Panoramic views atop the Berkshire Plateau
Strenuous	Road	No	Picturesque hilltop villages
Moderate	Road	Yes	Rolling farmland above Shelburne Falls
Strenuous	Hybrid	No	Miles of hidden dirt roads
Easy/Strenuous	Road	Yes/No	Well-preserved antique homes along "The Street"
Moderate	Road	No	The farmland that makes a dent in Connecticut
Easy	Road	Yes	Mount Sugarloaf
Easy to Moderate	Road	No	A scenic stretch of the Connecticut River
Moderate	Road	No	An agricultural valley
Moderate to Strenuous	Road	No	Country roads through a rural landscape

INTRODUCTION The rural part of Massachusetts that begins at the Connecticut River and stretches west through the Berkshire Hills is—for a cyclist—as close to perfection as one can get. This is a landscape more subtle than striking: a seemingly endless repetition of verdant rolling countryside, forested hills, patchwork farmland, and ridges that march northward in ever-increasing height to reach the foothills of the Green Mountains in Vermont and the Taconic Range in New York. Through it all is a network of scenic, lightly traveled back roads waiting for cyclists who wish to explore them.

When traveling by bike, a winding back road is a destination rather than a shortcut to someplace else. These routes were chosen for their scenic beauty, historical significance, and off the beaten path quality that make for the best cycling. They invite exploration and a stop in at a general store, a pause near a river, or a break in the shadow of an antique barn or ancient church.

Western Massachusetts is full of quiet Colonial villages blessedly untouched by progress. The best ones, like in Alford, Mount Washington, and Tyringham, have to be sought out. To get there, you must ride through an old-fashioned landscape of historic homesteads and farms tucked into hidden valleys and sitting on hilltops. Many of these places are remote and challenging to reach, but the reward is in finding a pristine enclave that most visitors have never seen.

I've divided western Massachusetts into four regions: the southern Berkshires, the northern Berkshires, the rugged and desolate Hampshire Hills to the east, and the rural villages and farmland along the Connecticut and Deerfield Rivers in the Pioneer Valley. Each has its own distinct flavor, which you'll find as you explore them.

Berkshire County sits at the far-western end of Massachusetts, running the full depth of the state from the northwest corner of Connecticut to the Green Mountains of southern Vermont. The long, rather low ridges of the southern Berkshires may lack the drama of New England's high craggy summits to the north, but the rolling hills seem to be everywhere, as either a panoramic backdrop or a challenging climb. Prim white houses line village greens, where you'll often find a general store or a Colonial church or a meetinghouse. The Housatonic River cuts a wide swath through the valley, furnishing water for farms and factories. The rides pass through villages whose names are synonymous with the Berkshires: Lee, Stockbridge, Great Barrington, Sheffield.

The Berkshires' verdant hills are dotted with working farms.

In the 19th century, the Berkshires became a popular summer retreat for high society. Business tycoons, politicians, and stars of the literary world and stage built opulent mansions, earning South County the nickname Newport North. An air of grandeur still prevails in villages like Lenox, where many of the estates are now exclusive inns and spas, museums, and performance venues.

The northern Berkshires are surrounded on three sides by rugged mountain ranges: the Taconics to the west, the foothills of the Green Mountains to the north, and the wildly remote Hoosac Range to the east. The area was dubbed the Berkshire Barrier because the steep ridges hindered trade and travel between western Massachusetts and the Pioneer Valley. Settlers eventually began to carve out an existence, building gristmills and sawmills, and planting orchards and raising livestock.

The Industrial Revolution made its way into the northern Berkshires in the 1800s. Massive brick, paper, and textile mills were built along rivers, blast furnaces and marble quarries in the hills. These small industries couldn't compete with westward expansion, however, and brick mill towns like North Adams and Adams became shadows of their former selves. Renovated mill buildings sprawl along the banks of the Housatonic and Hoosic Rivers; many working farms still thrive in these fertile lowlands.

Today, visitors flock to museums in Williamstown and North Adams, and summer theater and dance festivals in the hills. Others come to ski or kayak, as well as hike the Appalachian Trail or the path to the summit of Mount Greylock, the state's loftiest peak at 3,491 feet. Foliage burns brightly in autumn and draws throngs of tourists who come to witness the fiery display.

The remote and lofty Hampshire Hills make for challenging yet rewarding cycling through a pastoral landscape much like the New England of centuries ago. Remarkably, these scenic country lanes and historic villages attract relatively few visitors. Thick forest and upland meadows are crisscrossed by rambling stone walls and dotted with antique homesteads and the barns and silos of working farms. More than one hundred sugarhouses operate in these hills; when cycling in early spring, look for the telltale aluminum buckets clustered around the trunks of maple trees, waiting for warm days and cold nights to coax the sap to run.

The Connecticut River flows through the Pioneer Valley on its slow course from the Canadian border to Long Island Sound in southern Connecticut. The earliest settlers, thwarted by the state's rugged mountain ranges, planted crops in the fertile low-lands and plied the river on flat-bottomed boats for trade and travel between Greenfield and Northampton, and near other river communities. English settlers began farming Old Deerfield in 1669; today it's one of the country's best-preserved Colonial vil-lages. The valley's relatively gentle terrain makes for easier cycling than in the hill country to the west. Some of these rides stay close to the river; others snake through the valley's rich farmland and drift into the surrounding hills.

Keep in mind that Massachusetts is the nation's sixth smallest state. This book covers only the portion west of the Connecticut River—roughly 50 miles north to south and 65 miles from the New York border to the river. As a result, the rides are relatively close together, making it easy to explore routes from different areas. A few of the rides drift into Connecticut, New York, and Vermont, or over to the eastern bank of the Connecticut River.

The state population of 6.3 million is concentrated in the east-ern part of the state, leaving western Massachusetts generally serene. Its natural beauty is no secret, however, and hordes of tourists visit, especially during foliage season. Fortunately they tend not to stray far from two major arteries: US 7, cutting a swath north to south through Berkshire County; and the Mohawk Trail (MA 2), across northern Massachusetts from Williamstown to the Connecticut River. This leaves the back roads blissfully quiet and ready for cyclists to enjoy. It is easy to imagine when these roads were predated by a network of farm paths, trails, and dirt roads that wound through the hills from one village to the next. This is where the journey is more important than the desti-nation.

Western Massachusetts is crisscrossed with quiet country roads.

ABOUT THE RIDES This book is your guide to a variety of rides across western Massachusetts. Some explore a diverse landscape of farmland, forest, bustling mill towns, and remote hills—all in one route. Others will challenge you by climbing into the state's highest elevations. Some pass through Massachusetts's classic Colonial villages and college towns, and still others take hidden dirt roads through quiet woodland or follow the twisting course of a river through rugged terrain.

Distances range from a 9.5-mile ride loop around a scenic reservoir to a two-day tour of 117.2 miles through the Berkshires. Those looking for a challenge can test their mettle on the 8-mile climb to the summit of Mount Greylock; there is a chapter that covers the arduous route.

Read the tours carefully to decide which ones match your interests and ability. Information is provided on distance, terrain, difficulty, and recommended bicycle. Detailed route descriptions include the mileage at each road junction, but keep in mind that the mileage listed in the book might vary slightly from your own calculations since bike computers are calibrated differently. It's a good idea to pay attention to landmarks and signposts detailed in the ride description, as well as the mileage.

Each ride is designed to be completed in a day except for Ride 13: The Berkshire Hills. I've provided some lodging options for this ride; however, the area is crammed with bed & breakfasts and inns, so finding a place to stay is quite simple. It's still wise to call well ahead, especially during the foliage season and other peak travel times.

THE TERRAIN   Massachusetts was named after the Native Americans who first lived on the land. The name means large hill place, which hits home to cyclists familiar with the western part of the state.

Flat roads in western Massachusetts are rare; at best, the easiest routes in the river valleys have flat stretches connected by rolling hills. However, three of the state's major rivers—the Connecticut, Housatonic, and Hoosic—and other smaller rivers cut through the region; I tried to find back roads that follow their gentle lowland terrain to provide a respite in this area dominated by hills. In the Pioneer Valley, the routes along the Connecticut River have the flattest terrain. West of these lowlands is where the most challenging rides go deep into the hills between the Berkshire Valley and the Connecticut River, and the rugged Taconic Range on the state's extreme western border.

When pedaling around these rural areas, keep in mind that country roads are often narrow and winding with little or no shoulder to ride on. The beauty of these remote areas makes it easy to forget that you may be sharing the road with motorists who may not expect a cyclist to be around the corner, so remember to make yourself visible and ride predictably.

BICYCLE SAFETY   Wearing a helmet reduces the risk of a serious head injury by 85 percent in the event of an accident. Massachusetts state law requires children under 13 to wear one, but it's smart advice for anyone on a bike.

Be aware of your surroundings. Ride safely and responsibly by using hand signals to communicate with motorists and by riding in the same direction as traffic. Make yourself visible to drivers and pedestrians by using reflectors and wearing bright clothing, especially if riding at dusk. It's wise to maintain the assumption that motorists can't see you and to always be prepared for the unexpected, whether it's a car turning in front of you, a loose dog, or a hazard in the road.

Some of the routes pass through state forests or nature preserves that are laced with hiking trails; you will see the trailheads along the roads. Respect NO TRESPASSING signs and trails that prohibit cycling. Be considerate of hikers walking along the road in these areas; often people don't hear a bicycle when approached from behind, so make your presence known well in advance and leave as much room as possible when passing.

HELPFUL HINTS   It's every cyclist's responsibility to be self-sufficient at all times. Carry plenty of water and food, especially if there are no stores along the route. Know how to change or repair a flat tire, and bring along a spare tube, patch kit, air pump, and tire levers.

Before trying any of these routes, read the ride description and check the map so you know the area you're riding in, and note whether there are places for food and supplies along the way. When riding alone it's always a good idea to let someone know of your route and how long you plan to be out.

I highly recommend visiting the local bike shops near where you choose to ride; there are lists at the end of each chapter indicating the ones that are close to the route. Stop by before a ride to get supplies and advice on cycling in the area.

Planning ahead should include a careful inspection of your bike before each ride, paying attention to the following:

■ Check the tires for wear on the tread and sidewalls; add air if tire pressure is low.

- Replace brake pads and cables that are worn or frayed.
- Tighten the saddle and handlebars if they're loose.
- Spray lubricant on a dry or squeaky chain.
- Spin the tires and make adjustments if they wobble or rub against the brake pads.

If you're not comfortable doing this on your own, stop by a bike shop and have a mechanic take a look at your bike. Schedule a complete tune-up each spring, and keep your bike well maintained throughout the riding season.

FURTHER READING AND RESOURCES

Publications

Bicycling magazine
Box 7308
Red Oak, IA 51591-0308
1-800-666-2806
web site: www.bicyclingmagazine.com

The Ride magazine
678 Cortland Circle, Suite 16
Cheshire, CT 06410
e-mail: RideZine@aol.com
Publishes weekly club ride and race schedules and is sold in most bike shops.

Velo News magazine
1830 North 55th Street
Boulder, CO 80301-2700
web site: www.velonews.com

Massachusetts Atlas & Gazetteer
DeLorme Publishing Company
P.O. Box 298
Yarmouth, ME 04096
207-846-7000

*Provides topographical maps of Massachusetts in 71 detailed sections. The atlas
can be found in most bookstores around the state.*

Rubel BikeMaps
Box 401035
Cambridge, MA 02140
e-mail: info@bikemaps.com
web site: www.bikemaps.com
*Rubel's "Western Massachusetts Bicycle Map" is an invaluable supplement to the
routes in this book.*

Western Massachusetts Bicycle Clubs

Northampton Cycling Club
P.O. Box 886
Northampton, MA 01061
web site: www.northamptoncyclingclub.org

Berkshire Cycling Association
105 East Housatonic Street
Pittsfield, MA 01201
413-499-0462
web site: www.berkshirecycling.org
A racing and recreational cycling club for mountain and road cyclists.

Yankee Pedalers Cycling Club
web site: www.yankeepedalers.org
e-mail: yankpedal@aol.com

Franklin-Hampshire Freewheelers Cycling Club
413-548-9435
e-mail: Webmaster@Freewheelers.org
web site: www.freewheelers.org

Bicycling Organizations and Advocacy Groups

Massachusetts Bicycling Coalition (MassBike)
59 Temple Place #669
Boston, MA 02111
617-542-2453

web site: www.massbike.org
e-mail: bikeinfo@massbike.org
Statewide bicycling-advocacy organization that promotes cycling as a means of transportation, sponsors public events, supports educational initiatives, advocates for public bicycle projects, and promotes cycling-related legislation.

League of American Bicyclists
1612 K Street NW, Suite 401
Washington, D.C. 20006-2802
202-822-1333
e-mail: bikeleague@bikeleague.org
Promotes bicycling for fun, fitness, and transportation. Dedicated to advocacy, bike safety, and education at the local, state, and national levels. Founded as the League of American Wheelmen in 1880.

The Rails-to-Trails Conservancy
1100 17th Street (10th floor) NW
Washington, D.C. 20036
202-331-9696
web site: www.railtrails.org
A nonprofit public policy organization devoted to converting unused railroad lines into multiuse trails. The country's largest trails organization, trail building, advocacy, and public education group.

National Center for Bicycling & Walking
1506 21st Street NW, Suite 200
Washington, D.C. 20036
202-463-6622
web site: www.bikefed.org
e-mail: info@bikewalk.org
Founded as the Bicycle Federation of America, this national organization helps state and local cycling-advocacy groups to obtain federal funds for bike projects and helps federal agencies to develop bike-friendly policies and guidelines.

THE
SOUTHERN
BERKSHIRES

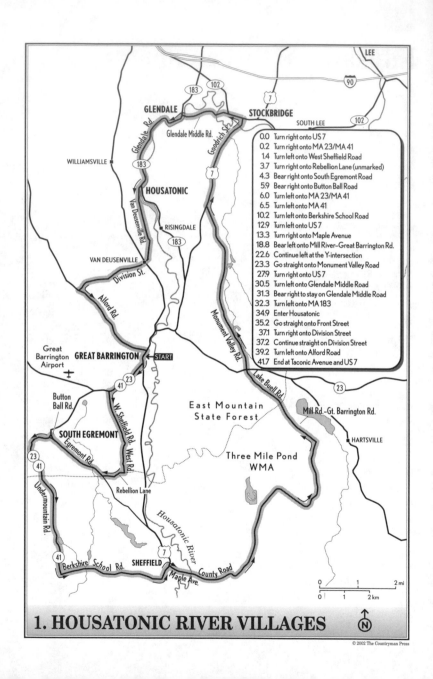

0.0 Turn right onto US 7
0.2 Turn right onto MA 23/MA 41
1.4 Turn left onto West Sheffield Road
3.7 Turn right onto Rebellion Lane (unmarked)
4.3 Bear right onto South Egremont Road
5.9 Bear right onto Button Ball Road
6.0 Turn left onto MA 23/MA 41
6.5 Turn left onto MA 41
10.2 Turn left onto Berkshire School Road
12.9 Turn left onto US 7
13.3 Turn right onto Maple Avenue
18.8 Bear left onto Mill River–Great Barrington Rd.
22.6 Continue left at the Y-intersection
23.3 Go straight onto Monument Valley Road
27.9 Turn right onto US 7
30.5 Turn left onto Glendale Middle Road
31.3 Bear right to stay on Glendale Middle Road
32.3 Turn left onto MA 183
34.9 Enter Housatonic
35.2 Go straight onto Front Street
37.1 Turn right onto Division Street
37.2 Continue straight on Division Street
39.2 Turn left onto Alford Road
41.7 End at Taconic Avenue and US 7

1. HOUSATONIC RIVER VILLAGES

© 2002 The Countryman Press

Housatonic River Villages

- **DISTANCE:** 41.7 miles
- **TERRAIN:** Low hills with flat stretches along the Housatonic River
- **DIFFICULTY:** Moderate to strenuous
- **RECOMMENDED BICYCLE:** Touring/road bike

This ride features the arts community of Great Barrington, the Colonial villages of South Egremont and Stockbridge, the antiques center of Sheffield, and the historic brick mill village of Housatonic, linked by back roads through scenic farm country. It is an ideal route for cyclists who want to tour Berkshire County without tackling its most rugged hills. Although the Berkshires march across this area, the roads meander through gently rolling farming valleys, consigning the peaks to a mere backdrop.

The route begins in one of the most culturally rich towns in the Berkshires. Great Barrington is a vibrant hub for the arts, from dance and theater to music and the visual arts. It's also a community of firsts: Main Street was the first in the nation to have electric lights, and the first armed resistance against the British took place near town hall, two years before the American Revolution began. Shops, cafés, and galleries line Main Street and make this town a good base for a tour through south Berkshire County.

The tiny village of South Egremont has the idyllic feel of a place long forgotten by time. The entire town center is a national historic landmark. Among the beautifully preserved Colonial buildings is the 1780 Egremont Inn, still open to the public after more than two hundred years.

In the 18th century, the final battle of Shays' Rebellion took place along one of these bucolic roadsides. Mobs of armed farmers organized by former Revolutionary War army captain Daniel Shays stormed courthouses across the state, protesting excessive taxes, adverse economic conditions, and the young nation's unstable currency. In February 1787 the rebels were captured just outside of South Egremont, sentenced to death for treason, and later pardoned.

A century later, the area's quiet beauty lured wealthy New York and Boston families to farms and estates to retreat to during the summer months. One of these estates, the 200-acre Great Pine Farm, is now the campus of Simon's Rock College of Bard.

The historic Merwin House on Main Street in Stockbridge

Philanthropist Elizabeth Blodgett Hall and her mother, Margaret Kendrick Blodgett, gave their family estate to start the country's first early college, an innovative concept offering a liberal arts education to highly motivated high school students ready for the academic rigors of college. It is the only school in the nation that offers young scholars the opportunity to become college students after the 10th grade.

The massive hulk of Monument Mountain can be seen along the road that bears its name. Novelists Nathaniel Hawthorne and Herman Melville were introduced on the mountain during an afternoon climb in 1850. Caught in a thunderstorm, they took shelter, drank champagne, and read William Cullen Bryant's poem *The Story of the Indian Girl*, based on the legend of a young woman who flung herself from the cliffs upon learning that the man she loved was killed in battle.

The hike marked the beginning of a long-standing literary and personal friendship: When Melville wrote *Moby-Dick* at his Pittsfield estate, he dedicated the opus to Hawthorne, who had his own summer retreat in Stockbridge.

Stockbridge is a quintessential New England village in the minds of its many visitors. Nearby, the tiny hamlet of Housatonic sits quietly off the beaten tourist path. A historic paper mill, a handful of art studios and galleries, a café, and a convenience store are in this village, which is named for the river that flows through it.

DIRECTIONS FOR THE RIDE

Start at the Southern Berkshire Chamber of Commerce, on the southern edge of downtown Great Barrington at the junction of US 7 and Taconic Avenue. There is parking behind the tiny white visitors center building. For food and supplies, head north on US 7 into downtown, or go south on US 7 toward Sheffield.

0.0 From the visitors center parking lot, turn right onto US 7 (Main Street). *This short stretch is busy with motorists and pedestrians, so use caution, especially when riding on weekends and holidays.*

0.2 At the first traffic light, turn right onto MA 23/41.

As you ride away from US 7, the road quickly becomes rural and open as it gently curves through a wide farming valley. The peaks of the Berkshires to the west provide a dramatic backdrop.

1.4 Turn left onto West Sheffield Road, following the green sign to the Wyantenuck Country Club.
Along this gradual ascent, the road narrows and passes several farm fields, a golf course, and a quiet neighborhood of historic homes before entering woods. The road surface becomes rough for about 1 mile through the forested section.

3.7 At the stop sign, turn right onto Rebellion Lane (unmarked).
Open meadows and scattered farm fields are flanked by the Berkshires along this peaceful rural road.

4.3 At the yield sign, bear right onto South Egremont Road.
Almost immediately you will pass a stone marker designating where the Appalachian Trail passes through a field and across the road on its 2,100-mile course from Springer Mountain, Georgia, to Mount Katahdin, Maine. A nearby sign marks the site of the final battle of Shays' Rebellion in February 1787.

5.9 In the village of South Egremont, bear right onto Button Ball Road.
This quiet New England village is a convergence of a couple rural roads flanked by historic Colonial buildings tucked behind neat white picket fences. The charming Egremont Inn has been the cornerstone of the village since 1780.

6.0 At the stop sign next to the tiny village green, turn left onto MA 23/41.

6.5 Turn left onto MA 41 (MA 23 continues straight).
There are good views of the Berkshires to the right, especially when you reach the crest of each rolling hill.

10.2 Turn left onto Berkshire School Road.

12.9 At the stop sign, turn left onto US 7, into Sheffield.

13.3 Turn right onto Maple Avenue (which turns to County Road at the junction with Hewins Street).

18.8 At the Y-intersection, bear left onto Mill River–Great Barrington Road.

22.6 At the next Y-intersection, continue left.

23.3 At the stop sign, go straight onto Monument Valley Road, crossing MA 23.

Along this road you'll catch occasional glimpses of the open rocky face of Monument Mountain straight ahead. The distinctive quartzite ridge—also known as Squaw Peak—rises 1,700 feet above the valley floor.

27.9 At the stop sign, turn right onto US 7.

30.5 At the stop sign in Stockbridge, turn left onto Glendale Middle Road (US 7 continues to the right here, at the Red Lion Inn).
Stockbridge was founded in 1734 by a handful of white settlers and their families. Members of the local Mohegan tribe served in the American Revolution—the only Native Americans to do so—and were the first to become U.S. citizens. The massive white clapboard Red Lion Inn on the corner is a New England icon, depicted in Norman Rockwell's infamous painting Main Street Stockbridge. *On Main Street, the Merwin House is a restored 1825 summer home; nearby is the Mission House, built in 1739 by John Sergeant, the first missionary sent to educate the local Mohegan tribe. Farther down the road, the quiet village green is flanked by 19th-century buildings, including the grand pillared town hall, the handsome brick Congregational Church, and the Field Chime Tower.*

31.3 After crossing the metal bridge, bear right to stay on Glendale Middle Road.

32.3 At the stop sign, turn left onto MA 183.
This scenic, gently rolling stretch follows the Housatonic River.

34.9 Enter the village of Housatonic.
Rambling brick factory buildings, a railroad station, an art gallery, restored mill houses, and a café fill this former mill village.

35.2 At the southern tip of the village, go straight onto Front Street (MA 183 makes a left turn here, passing under a railroad bridge).

37.1 At the white church (Guthrie Center), turn right onto Division Street.

37.2 At the blinking red light, cross MA 41 and continue straight on Division Street.

39.2 Turn left onto Alford Road.
The campus of Simon's Rock College of Bard is at the last climb before descending into Great Barrington.

41.7 The ride ends at the chamber of commerce building on Taconic Avenue and US 7 in downtown Great Barrington.

Bicycle Shops

Berkshire Bike & Blade, 326 Stockbridge Road (US 7), Great Barrington; 413-528-5555

Foster Harland Inc., 15 Bridge Street, Great Barrington; 413-528-0564

2

The Berkshires to the Twin Lakes

- **DISTANCE:** 35.7 miles
- **TERRAIN:** Flat with some rolling hills and two moderately steep climbs; a 1-mile dirt road
- **DIFFICULTY:** Moderate
- **RECOMMENDED BICYCLE:** Touring/road bike

For the southern Berkshires, this ride is relatively flat with a few exceptions: a couple moderate climbs and some sections of rolling hills. For cyclists who want to explore the Berkshires without the challenging climbs, this is an ideal route. Some of the roads follow the Housatonic River as it flows through rural farmland, and then dip below the Connecticut border, where they skirt around the Twin Lakes in Salisbury. For the most part, the hills provide a dramatic backdrop instead of the way to go.

Great Barrington, an eclectic town surrounded by farmland and forest, is referred to by some as the metropolis of South County. Its shops, galleries, and cafés make it an interesting place to explore after the ride.

South Egremont sits beneath the towering hills of Mount Washington State Forest, which borders the rugged Taconic Range. The village is named for Charles Windham, Earl of Egremont, the British secretary of state during the American Revolution. The Old Academy is a neat white building housing the town offices, grange, and library; it is next to an old burial ground. Main Street is lined

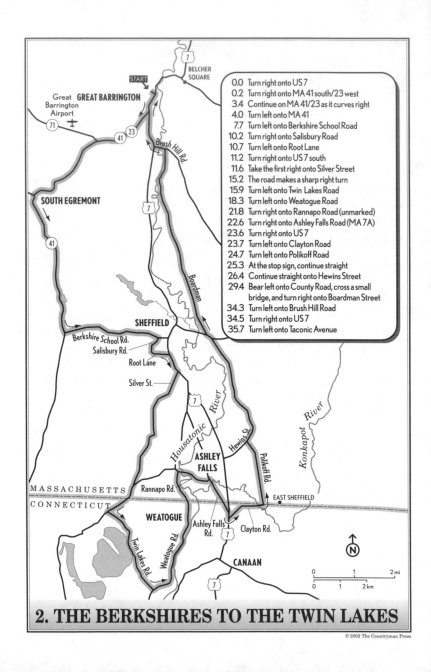

START

BELCHER SQUARE

Great **GREAT BARRINGTON**
Great
Barrington
Airport

Brush Hill Rd.

SOUTH EGREMONT

Boardman

SHEFFIELD

Berkshire School Rd.
Salisbury Rd.
Root Lane
Silver St.

Housatonic River

Konkapot River

ASHLEY FALLS

Hewins St.

Polikoff Rd.

M A S S A C H U S E T T S

C O N N E C T I C U T

Rannapo Rd.

EAST SHEFFIELD

WEATOGUE

Ashley Falls
Rd.

Clayton Rd.

Twin Lakes Rd.

Weatogue Rd.

CANAAN

0.0   Turn right onto US 7
0.2   Turn right onto MA 41 south/23 west
3.4   Continue on MA 41/23 as it curves right
4.0   Turn left onto MA 41
7.7   Turn left onto Berkshire School Road
10.2 Turn right onto Salisbury Road
10.7 Turn left onto Root Lane
11.2 Turn right onto US 7 south
11.6 Take the first right onto Silver Street
15.2 The road makes a sharp right turn
15.9 Turn left onto Twin Lakes Road
18.3 Turn left onto Weatogue Road
21.8 Turn right onto Rannapo Road (unmarked)
22.6 Turn right onto Ashley Falls Road (MA 7A)
23.6 Turn right onto US 7
23.7 Turn left onto Clayton Road
24.7 Turn left onto Polikoff Road
25.3 At the stop sign, continue straight
26.4 Continue straight onto Hewins Street
29.4 Bear left onto County Road, cross a small
       bridge, and turn right onto Boardman Street
34.3 Turn left onto Brush Hill Road
34.5 Turn right onto US 7
35.7 Turn left onto Taconic Avenue

N

0   1   2 mi
0   1   2 km

2. THE BERKSHIRES TO THE TWIN LAKES

with galleries, antiques shops, and cafés that lead to a tiny green and the Egremont Inn, a double-porched rambling inn that has resided at the edge of the village since 1780.

Berkshire County's oldest house is in the village of Ashley Falls. Colonel John Ashley designed and built the clapboard home for his family in 1735. The Yale graduate, lawyer, and entrepreneur became a colonel during the French and Indian War. The Sheffield Declaration, which condemned British tyranny and advocated equal property rights, was drafted in the second-floor study of his house in 1773. The document is considered the forerunner of the Declaration of Independence and proclaimed that "mankind in a State of Nature are equal, free, and independent of each other and have a right to the undisturbed Enjoyment of their Lives, their Liberty, and Property." Ashley's black slave Mum Bett was the first to win freedom after the Revolution under the state's new constitution.

Also in Ashley Falls is Bartholomew's Cobble, named for the marble and quartzite outcroppings that rise 100 feet above rural pastureland near the Connecticut border. The nature preserve is maintained by the Trustees of Reservations, a state group that preserves and maintains historic and natural properties. The preserve is home to more than 200 species of birds, 740 species of plants, and 45 species of ferns, making it one of the nation's largest concentrations of ferns.

DIRECTIONS FOR THE RIDE

The ride begins in Great Barrington at the Southern Berkshire Chamber of Commerce, just south of downtown on US 7 at Taconic Avenue. Parking is located behind the tiny white building.

0.0 Turn right out of the visitors center parking lot onto US 7.
This is a congested area, especially on weekends, so use caution.

0.2 At the traffic light, turn right onto MA 41 south/23 west.
Along this country road to Egremont there are spectacular views of the Berkshire Hills behind rolling farm fields.

3.4 Immediately after passing through South Egremont, be sure to continue on MA 41/23 as it curves to the right.
You can pick up food and drinks in this classic Colonial village.

Cycling is a pleasure on the back roads of the southern Berkshires.

4.0 Turn left onto MA 41, following signs toward Salisbury and Lakeville, Connecticut.
MA 41 is a quiet country road that follows the ridgeline that rolls south toward Connecticut. Notice the handsome early-American homesteads surrounded by miles of farmland. The road is rolling but mostly downhill.

7.3 Pass the sprawling campus of the Berkshire School.
This prestigious private school for boys on the lower slopes of Mount Everett was established in 1907 by Seaver Buck. Originally housed in three farmhouses and two barns, it has grown into a collection of stately brick buildings.

7.7 Turn left onto Berkshire School Road, following the sign for US 7.

10.2 Turn right onto Salisbury Road.

10.7 Turn left onto Root Lane.
Salisbury Road curves to the right here.

11.2 At the stop sign, turn right onto US 7 south.

11.6 Take the first right onto Silver Street.
At the end of Silver Street, there is a tiny park with a memorial stone marking the site of the elm tree that is featured on the town seal. Its history is rich: Sheffield's first white settler camped beneath it in the early 18th century, and later it was the site of town gatherings. It was believed to be about four hundred years old—the trunk was 20 feet in diameter—when it was cut in 1926.

14.8 At the crest of Cooper Hill Road, stop and look back for one of the ride's most panoramic views.

15.2 Follow the road as it makes a sharp right turn, and continue descending into Salisbury, Connecticut.

15.9 Turn left onto Twin Lakes Road.
This narrow road twists through the woods past summer cottages on the shore of beautiful Lake Washining (East Twin Lake).

18.3 At the T-intersection, turn left onto Weatogue Road.
There is a good view here of Canaan Mountain to the right. The road follows the Housatonic River and the farms and fields that flank the river.

21.0 Cross back into Massachusetts.
Look for a small stone marker designating the state line. The road turns to hard-packed dirt here for less than 1 mile.

21.6 On the left, you will pass the trailhead for Bartholomew's Cobble.
The Trustees of Reservations oversees this 270-acre tract along the Housatonic River.

21.8 Turn right onto Rannapo Road (unmarked).
To the left is a sign for the Colonel Ashley House. John Ashley built this handsome oak and chestnut farmhouse for his family in 1735. Tours of the antiques-filled house are led on weekends and select days from Memorial Day through Columbus Day.

22.6 At the stop sign and blinking red light, turn right onto Ashley Falls Road (MA 7A).
Ashley Falls sits near the confluence of the Housatonic and Konkapot Rivers. The village's namesake falls are at the site of an old stone dam on the Konkapot River.

The stone quarries that once lined the river provided much of the marble for the courthouse in New York and the customhouse in Boston, among many other urban buildings.

23.3 Cross into Canaan, Connecticut.

23.6 At the stop sign, turn right onto US 7.

23.7 Turn left just after the Connecticut State Police barracks onto Clayton Road.
This winding flat road will take you away from the busy highway and past homes, farms, and produce stands.

24.7 Turn left onto Polikoff Road.
This intersection is just after crossing the Konkapot River.

25.3 At the stop sign, continue straight.

26.4 At the stop sign, continue straight onto Hewins Street, crossing Alum Hill Road.
You will pass the flat, groomed fields of a turf farm, then gradually climb into the woods, with nice views of the Berkshires to the left.

29.4 At the stop sign, bear left onto County Road, cross a small bridge, and then take an immediate right onto Boardman Street.
You will pass some beautifully restored Colonial homesteads and farms. The road will eventually narrow and once again follow the Housatonic River.

34.3 Turn left onto Brush Hill Road.

34.5 At the stop sign, turn right onto US 7.
Follow US 7 north to return to Great Barrington.

35.7 At the traffic light, turn left onto Taconic Avenue, and then immediately left into the visitors center parking lot to end the ride.

Bicycle Shops

Berkshire Bike & Blade, 326 Stockbridge Road (US 7), Great Barrington; 413-528-5555

Foster Harland Inc., 15 Bridge Street, Great Barrington; 413-528-0564

3

Stockbridge

- **DISTANCE**: 28.8 miles
- **TERRAIN**: Rolling terrain with a few moderate climbs; about 3 miles of dirt roads
- **DIFFICULTY**: Moderate
- **RECOMMENDED BICYCLE**: Touring/road bike

One of the best-known landmarks in Stockbridge—and perhaps in New England—is the rambling white clapboard, 18th-century Red Lion Inn. Anyone traveling through this quintessential Colonial village on US 7 passes its inviting wide porches filled with rocking chairs. It was built in 1773 by Silas Pepoon as a tavern and stage-coach stop on the Boston to Albany route. The present Victorian building was erected on the site after the original hotel burned in 1896. Norman Rockwell's painting *Main Street Stockbridge* featured the inn and made it a symbol of New England. Its guest list includes several presidents as well as literary icons from the area, such as William Cullen Bryant, Nathaniel Hawthorne, and Henry Wadsworth Longfellow, who all visited in the 1800s.

Stockbridge was known as Indian Town when it became the new home for local Housatonic Indians after investors purchased a wide tract of land along the river in 1722. Relations with English settlers were peaceful at first; many converted to Christianity and adopted English ways. During the French and Indian War, Stockbridge Indians fought alongside the English army.

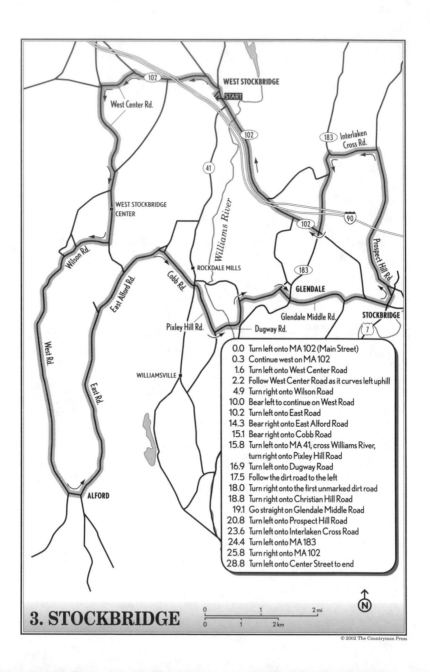

West Center Rd.

WEST STOCKBRIDGE

102

START

102

183 Interlaken Cross Rd.

41

Williams River

90

102

WEST STOCKBRIDGE CENTER

Wilson Rd.

East Alford Rd.

Cobb Rd.

ROCKDALE MILLS

183

Prospect Hill Rd.

GLENDALE

STOCKBRIDGE

Glendale Middle Rd.

West Rd.

East Rd.

Pixley Hill Rd.

Dugway Rd.

7

WILLIAMSVILLE

0.0 Turn left onto MA 102 (Main Street)
0.3 Continue west on MA 102
1.6 Turn left onto West Center Road
2.2 Follow West Center Road as it curves left uphill
4.9 Turn right onto Wilson Road
10.0 Bear left to continue on West Road
10.2 Turn left onto East Road
14.3 Bear right onto East Alford Road
15.1 Bear right onto Cobb Road
15.8 Turn left onto MA 41, cross Williams River, turn right onto Pixley Hill Road
16.9 Turn left onto Dugway Road
17.5 Follow the dirt road to the left
18.0 Turn right onto the first unmarked dirt road
18.8 Turn right onto Christian Hill Road
19.1 Go straight on Glendale Middle Road
20.8 Turn left onto Prospect Hill Road
23.6 Turn left onto Interlaken Cross Road
24.4 Turn left onto MA 183
25.8 Turn right onto MA 102
28.8 Turn left onto Center Street to end

ALFORD

3. STOCKBRIDGE

0   1   2 mi
0   1   2 km

N

The 1739 Mission House on Main Street was the Reverend John Sergeant's home and headquarters for his work as the first missionary to the Stockbridge Indians. From June through Columbus Day, visitors can view the clapboard house and its 18th-century furnishings. On the village green you will find the Field Chime Tower, erected in 1870s on the site of the old Indian meetinghouse; the 1824 First Congregational Church, a handsome redbrick building with a classic Colonial white steeple; and the cemetery where Reverend Sergeant is buried along with some of the Indians he converted. After Sergeant's death, the Indians migrated from their ancestral home, moving first to New York before eventually settling in Wisconsin.

Hidden on a quiet dirt road in the Glendale section of Stockbridge is Chesterwood, the 160-acre estate of sculptor Daniel Chester French. Among his best-known works are the seated statue in Washington's Lincoln Memorial and the statue *Minute Man* in Concord. The internationally acclaimed artist summered here from 1897 to 1931. The grand home, gardens, and studio are open to visitors from May through October.

Another Stockbridge estate is open to summer visitors. Naumkeag sits atop Prospect Hill, one of many opulent late-19th-century and early 20th-century mansions overlooking the village. The 26-room, rambling shingled house was built in 1886 for Joseph Hodges Choate, an illustrious attorney and ambassador to the Court of St. James under President McKinley. Named for the Mahican word meaning haven of peace, the estate features exquisitely designed terraced gardens, a reflecting pool, and a walled Chinese garden.

The ride also passes by Berkshire Botanical Garden, a 15-acre oasis of herbs, perennials, ponds, and trails founded in 1934. Down the road is the Norman Rockwell Museum, housed in an estate on the Housatonic River. The venerable illustrator of American people and events moved to Stockbridge in 1953, where he remained until his death 25 years later. The museum houses two hundred of his works, from the infamous *Saturday Evening Post* covers to his other illustrations that chronicled everyday American life and world events, from World War II to space flight.

It is the largest collection and only permanent exhibition of Rockwell's original paintings.

West Stockbridge is a quiet roadside village close to the New York border, an eclectic jumble of artists' studios and galleries, cafés, and shops that is a relaxed contrast to the well-manicured estates and historic sites of Stockbridge. Even farther afield is Alford, a Colonial village in an isolated valley that seems to have slipped out of the mainstream of 20th-century America.

DIRECTIONS FOR THE RIDE
The ride starts in the center of West Stockbridge. Park in the municipal lot at the end of Center Street, across from the post office.

0.0 Follow Center Street into the village and turn left onto MA 102 (Main Street).

0.3 Continue west on MA 102 at the junction of MA 41.

1.6 Turn left onto West Center Road.
Farm fields stretch in all directions in this rural valley dotted with barns and bordered by the Taconic Range.

2.2 Follow West Center Road as it curves uphill to the left; this is at the junction of Woodruff Road.

4.9 Turn right onto Wilson Road, which will turn into West Road as you cross the Alford town line.
This flat, beautiful country road is lined with farms and antique homes.

10.0 Bear left to continue on West Road; North Egremont Road will be on the right.

10.2 In the center of Alford, turn left onto East Road.
This tiny village of tidy white clapboard buildings is typical of New England a couple hundred years ago and remains much like the town was when settled in 1750. It was an agricultural community that supported a tannery, iron furnace and forge, and several sawmills, gristmills, and marble quarries.

14.3 At the Y-intersection, bear right onto East Alford Road.
Use caution as the road winds downhill.

15.1 Near the bottom of the hill, bear right onto Cobb Road.

15.8 At the stop sign, turn left onto MA 41, cross over the Williams River, and then take an immediate right onto Pixley Hill Road.
This unpaved but well-surfaced road climbs into the hills.

16.9 At the top of the hill, turn left onto Dugway Road.
Use caution on the descent. The road will become paved as you cross into Stockbridge.

17.5 At the sign for Pixley Hill Road, follow the dirt road to the left.

18.0 Turn right onto the first unmarked dirt road.
This road takes you past Chesterwood, the opulent summer estate of sculptor Daniel Chester French.

18.8 Just past the Chesterwood estate, turn right onto Christian Hill Road.

Shops along historic Main Street in Stockbridge

19.1 At the stop sign, go straight on Glendale Middle Road, crossing MA 183.
This leads to historic Main Street in Stockbridge.

20.8 In the center of Stockbridge, turn left at the Red Lion Inn onto Prospect Hill Road.
In about 0.25 mile you'll come to a Y-intersection; stay to the left and climb up the hill past the Naumkeag estate.

23.6 Turn left onto Interlaken Cross Road.

24.4 Turn left onto MA 183.

25.8 At the blinking red light, turn right onto MA 102.
Berkshire Botanical Garden is on the left just past the intersection.

28.8 In West Stockbridge, turn left onto Center Street to end the ride.

Bicycle Shops

Berkshire Bike & Blade, 326 Stockbridge Road (US 7), Great Barrington; 413-528-5555

Foster Harland Inc., 15 Bridge Street, Great Barrington; 413-528-0564

The Arcadian Shop, 91 Pittsfield Road (US 7), Lenox; 1-800-239-3391

Mean Wheels Bike Shop, 57A Housatonic Street, Lenox; 413-637-0644

4

Great Barrington to New York

- **DISTANCE:** 27.4 miles
- **TERRAIN:** Flat stretches, rolling hills, one steep climb; a 2-mile dirt road
- **DIFFICULTY:** Strenuous
- **RECOMMENDED BICYCLE:** Touring/road bike

This backcountry ride tours the rural outskirts of Great Barrington, dips into New York via the Taconic Range, and then passes through the classic crossroads village of South Egremont. This is a relatively gentle landscape of farmland and rolling hills that becomes more rugged as you near the state line.

The largest town in the southern Berkshires is a convenient base for riding and offers many post-ride activities that will encourage you to stay. No matter what time of year you ride here, there are numerous cultural activities in the area, from dance and theater to musical performances and art exhibitions. The Berkshire Opera Company hosts its summer festival in the historic Mahaiwe Theatre—a former vaudeville house—on Castle Street. There are a number of good ethnic restaurants downtown.

When Indians occupied the area between Great Barrington and Stockbridge, it was known as Happy Valley and served as the Indian capital of the Housatonic lowlands. The largest congregation of Indians lived in this area, and many of their graves are where the buildings of Great Barrington's Main Street now stand,

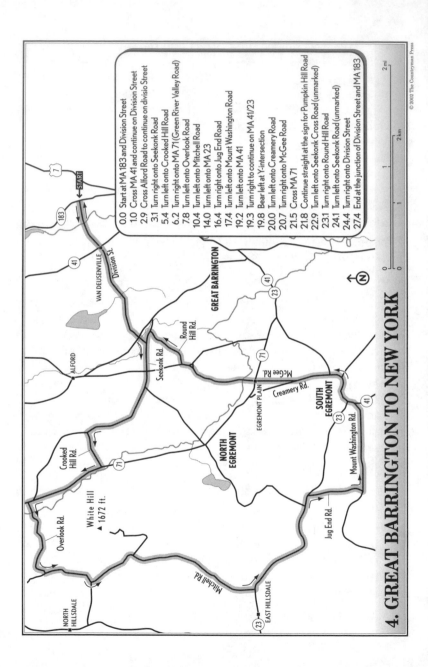

4. GREAT BARRINGTON TO NEW YORK

0.0   Start at MA 183 and Division Street
1.0   Cross MA 41 and continue on Division Street
2.9   Cross Alford Road to continue on divisio Street
3.1   Turn right onto Seekonk Road
5.4   Turn left onto Crooked Hill Road
6.2   Turn right onto MA 71 (Green River Valley Road)
7.8   Turn left onto Overlook Road
10.4 Turn left onto Mitchell Road
14.0 Turn left onto MA 23
16.4 Turn left onto Jug End Road
17.4 Turn left onto Mount Washington Road
19.2 Turn left onto MA 41
19.3 Turn right to continue on MA 41/23
19.8 Bear left at Y-intersection
20.0 Turn left onto Creamery Road
20.7 Turn right onto McGee Road
21.5 Cross MA 71
21.8 Continue straight at the sign for Pumpkin Hill Road
22.9 Turn left onto Seekonk Cross Road (unmarked)
23.1 Turn right onto Round Hill Road
24.1 Turn left onto Seekonk Road (unmarked)
24.4 Turn right onto Division Street
27.4 End at the junction of Division Street and MA 183

© 2002 The Countryman Press

between the east side of Main Street and the west bank of the Housatonic River.

The historic Egremont Inn, the three-story, double-porched, white clapboard inn at the heart of South Egremont, was a busy stage-coach stop in the late 1700s. During the Civil War it served as the town hall and hospital. The hearth in the living room was once a blacksmith's forge. The village is among the most noted and lovely in the Berkshires, lined with neat white houses. The final scene of Shays' Rebellion was played out here after the Revolution. Angry war veterans and local farmers protested against the area's wealthy aristocrats and threatened to take over the Springfield armory. The grievances over unfair tax and property laws—their property was being seized by government for failure to pay back taxes—led to violent rebellion. About one hundred rebels and their hostages fought the Sheffield militia. The militia won, and Shays was captured.

The influx of artists, writers, and wealthy summer visitors changed the face of the Berkshires in the 19th century and continues to influence the area today. Those looking for a rich cultural life and beautiful natural surroundings retreat to grand country homes in the hills between Great Barrington and New York. Farmers continue to make their living in the area.

DIRECTIONS FOR THE RIDE

The ride starts in Great Barrington at the junction of MA 183 and Division Street, just north of downtown. There is a market and deli in South Egremont and several food stores in Great Barrington.

0.0 Start at MA 183 and Division Street.
The ride begins with an easy flat stretch of road through a quiet area that once bustled with mills and factories.

1.0 At the blinking red light, cross MA 41 and continue on Division Street.

2.9 At the stop sign, cross Alford Road to continue on Division Street.

3.1 At the stop sign, turn right onto Seekonk Road.

5.4 Turn left onto Crooked Hill Road.
This rolling country road offers spectacular views from the top, making the effort worth it; enjoy the views on the descent.

A sprawling sheep farm in Great Barrington

6.2 At the stop sign, turn right onto MA 71 (Green River Valley Road).
The state line and the town of Hillsdale are about 0.5 mile up this main road that follows the Green River into New York.

7.8 Turn left onto Overlook Road.
This semi-paved road winds uphill for about 1.5 miles through the woods, making it this route's most challenging climb; you will be rewarded for your efforts with sweeping views on the other side. The steep descent will bring you quickly to the valley floor.

10.4 At the T-intersection, turn left onto Mitchell Road.
This quiet rural road begins at the base of the hill at Skarship Farm. This is a bucolic region of patchwork green fields and wooded hills dotted with the barns and silos of working farms.

14.0 At the stop sign, turn left onto MA 23.
You will be back in Massachusetts in about 1 mile. The steep slopes of Catamount Ski Area straddle the state line.

16.4 Turn right onto Jug End Road, following signs for Bash Bish Falls and Mount Washington State Forest.

17.4 At the stop sign, turn left onto Mount Washington Road.

19.2 At the stop sign, turn left onto MA 41.

19.3 At the next stop sign, turn right to continue on MA 41/23.
This road will take you into the village of South Egremont.

19.8 At the Y-intersection in South Egremont, bear left to pass by the tiny village green behind the Egremont Inn.

20.0 Just past the village, turn left onto Creamery Road (MA 23/41 curves to the right).

20.7 Turn right onto McGee Road.

21.5 At the stop sign, cross MA 71.
Maps refer to this road collectively as Hill Road, Locust Hill Road, and Pumpkin Hill Road.

21.8 When you see West Plain Road, go to the right; continue straight at the sign for Pumpkin Hill Road.
These are some of the most beautiful rural roads in the southern Berkshires.

22.9 Turn left onto Seekonk Cross Road (unmarked).
Here you will ride past a sprawling sheep farm.

23.1 At the edge of the sheep pasture, turn right onto Round Hill Road.

24.1 At the stop sign, turn left onto Seekonk Road (unmarked).

24.4 Turn right onto Division Street.

27.4 The ride ends at the junction of Division Street and MA 183.

Bicycle Shops

Berkshire Bike & Blade, 326 Stockbridge Road (US 7), Great Barrington; 413-528-5555

Foster Harland Inc., 15 Bridge Street, Great Barrington; 413-528-0564

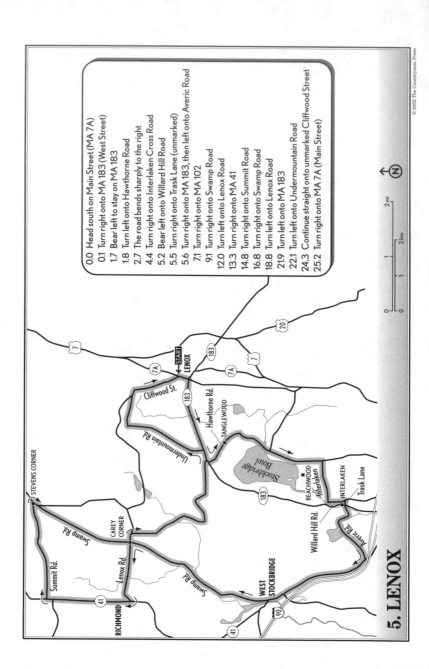

5. LENNOX

0.0 Head south on Main Street (MA 7A)
0.1 Turn right onto MA 183 (West Street)
1.7 Bear left to stay on MA 183
1.8 Turn left onto Hawthorne Road
2.7 The road bends sharply to the right
4.4 Turn right onto Interlaken Cross Road
5.2 Bear left onto Willard Hill Road
5.5 Turn right onto Trask Lane (unmarked)
5.6 Turn right onto MA 183, then left onto Averic Road
7.1 Turn right onto MA 102
9.1 Turn right onto Swamp Road
12.0 Turn left onto Lenox Road
13.3 Turn right onto MA 41
14.8 Turn right onto Summit Road
16.8 Turn right onto Swamp Road
18.8 Turn left onto Lenox Road
21.9 Turn left onto MA 183
22.1 Turn left onto Undermountain Road
24.3 Continue straight onto unmarked Cliffwood Street
25.2 Turn right onto MA 7A (Main Street)

5

Lenox

- **DISTANCE:** 25.2 miles
- **TERRAIN:** Gradual to moderately rolling hills with steeper terrain over Lenox Mountain; a 1-mile dirt road
- **DIFFICULTY:** Moderate
- **RECOMMENDED BICYCLE:** Touring/road bike

The ride begins in the elegant old resort town of Lenox and follows winding back roads through wooded hills and rural farmland before crossing Lenox Mountain to return to the village. Along the way you'll pass by a world-class summer music festival, Colonial villages, and a forested wildlife sanctuary.

In the 19th century, this is where the Berkshires' wealthy elite summered in opulent mansions and on gentrified farms. Many of these estates are privately owned, while others have been converted into private schools, exclusive inns and spas, and performance venues.

One of them is Tanglewood, the former 210-acre estate of William Aspinwall Tappan that became the summer home of the Boston Symphony Orchestra in 1937. Today, well-heeled audiences pack elegant picnics and listen to classical, jazz, and chamber recitals and performances by the Boston Pops.

Stockbridge Bowl is a beautiful lake that rests in the hills between Lenox and Stockbridge. Local Indians named it Mahkeenac, meaning Great Water. The Great Josh Billings Triathlon has been an annual fall event here for more than 25 years. Participants bicycle to the Bowl from Great Barrington, canoe across the lake, and finally run around it. Josh Billings is the pen name of 19th-century humorist and Lanesborough native Henry Wheeler Shaw, whose favorite saying was "to finish is to win." It has been adopted as the motto of this bike-canoe-run triathlon, the oldest and largest such competition in the nation.

Hawthorne Cottage is a reproduction of the rambling red cottage overlooking Stockbridge Bowl where Nathaniel Hawthorne lived with his family in the 19th century. The National Federation of Music Clubs built the replica after the original structure was destroyed by fire. Hawthorne's most creative period was when he lived in Lenox. He wrote *The House of the Seven Gables* here in

Hawthorne Cottage sits in wooded hills above Stockbridge Bowl.

1850, as well as *Tanglewood Tales*, a collection of nature stories inspired by his rural surroundings.

The village of West Stockbridge is relaxed and eclectic compared to the formality of Lenox. The 1788 Center Church, with its graceful and towering steeple, is regarded as one of the finest in the Berkshires. Interlaken has several restored buildings, including the ornate Victorian Citizens Hall. The Pleasant Valley Wildlife Sanctuary is a 730-acre Massachusetts Audubon Society preserve on Lenox Mountain, home to a diverse population of birds and animals, including an active beaver colony.

DIRECTIONS FOR THE RIDE

The ride begins on MA 7A (Main Street) in Lenox. Park on Main Street in front of a small park at Main and Cliffwood Streets (across from a Mobil gas station and O'Brien's Market) or in the nearby Village Center shopping plaza.

0.0 Head south on Main Street (MA 7A) into the center of Lenox.

0.1 At the stop sign, turn right onto MA 183 (West Street).

1.7 Where the road splits, bear left to stay on MA 183, passing the Kripalu Center for Yoga and Health.
This yoga-based holistic health center is the largest such facility in the country. The sprawling brick complex is on the site of Andrew Carnegie's former Shadowbrook estate overlooking the Stockbridge Bowl. Carnegie's grand mansion—the country's largest private home in its time—was destroyed by fire in 1956.

1.8 Just past the main entrance for Tanglewood, turn left onto Hawthorne Road.
This narrow country road has sweeping views of the Berkshire Hills and Stockbridge Bowl. Hawthorne Cottage sits at the edge of a high field above the lake.

2.7 Follow the road as it bends sharply to the right, which changes into Mahkeenac Road (unmarked).
Wheatleigh is on the left as you make the turn. The elegant Florentine palazzo built of yellow brick in 1893 is now a gracious resort. The road winds downhill, flattens as it hugs the lakeshore, and then climbs away from the Bowl.

4.4 Turn right onto Interlaken Cross Road.

5.2 At the Y-intersection, bear left onto Willard Hill Road.
This quiet road will take you through Interlaken, a sleepy hamlet that is part of Stockbridge. Notice the handsome brick church and Interlaken Art School, surrounded by well-preserved antique homes.

5.5 Turn right at the sign for Hill Road onto Trask Lane (unmarked).

5.6 Turn right onto MA 183, then take an immediate left onto Averic Road.
In about 0.5 mile, the pavement gives way to a well-groomed dirt road, which winds uphill into the woods.

7.1 Turn right and follow MA 102 into West Stockbridge.
Main Street is lined with cafés, shops, and galleries, including a variety store if you need supplies.

9.1 In the village center, turn right onto Swamp Road.

12.0 At the blinking yellow light, turn left onto Lenox Road.

13.3 At the stop sign, turn right onto MA 41.

14.8 Just past the junction of MA 295, turn right onto Summit Road.

16.8 At the stop sign, turn right onto Swamp Road.

18.8 At the blinking yellow light, turn left onto Lenox Road.
There is a considerable amount of climbing on this part of the ride, first through farm fields, then into the wooded hills of the Yokun Ridge Forest Reservation. At the crest of the hill is an overlook with a good spot to rest and enjoy dramatic views of the Stockbridge Bowl before beginning the descent into Lenox.

21.9 At the stop sign, turn left onto MA 183.

22.1 Turn left onto Undermountain Road.
This beautiful back road skirts a farm valley at the base of Lenox Mountain. The forested hills are part of the 730-acre Pleasant Valley Wildlife Sanctuary, maintained by the Massachusetts Audubon Society. It also includes meadows and wetlands that provide a rich habitat to 80 species of birds and a beaver colony.

24.3 Where you see Reservoir Road on the left, continue straight onto unmarked Cliffwood Street.

25.2 At the stop sign, turn right onto MA 7A/Main Street to end the ride.

Bicycle Shops

The Arcadian Shop, 91 Pittsfield Road (US 7), Lenox; 1-800-239-3391

Main Street Sports & Leisure, 48 Main Street (MA 7A), Lenox; 413-637-4407

Mean Wheels Bike Shop, 57A Housatonic Street, Lenox; 413-637-0644

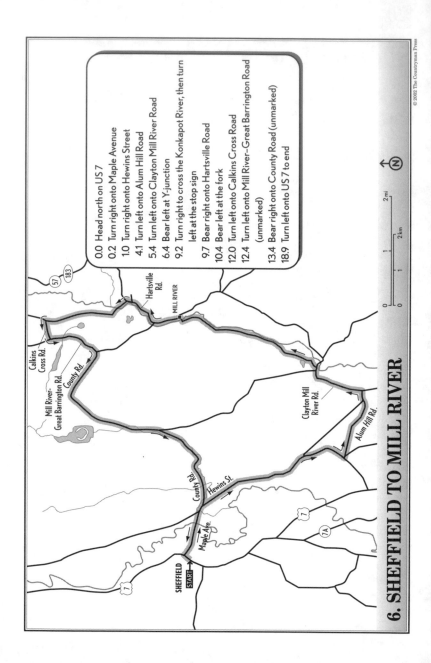

6. SHEFFIELD TO MILL RIVER

0.0 Head north on US 7

0.2 Turn right onto Maple Avenue

1.0 Turn right onto Hewins Street

4.1 Turn left onto Alum Hill Road

5.4 Turn left onto Clayton Mill River Road

6.4 Bear left at Y-junction

9.2 Turn right to cross the Konkapot River, then turn left at the stop sign

9.7 Bear right onto Hartsville Road

10.4 Bear left at the fork

12.0 Turn left onto Calkins Cross Road

12.4 Turn left onto Mill River–Great Barrington Road (unmarked)

13.4 Bear right onto County Road (unmarked)

18.9 Turn left onto US 7 to end

© 2002 The Countryman Press

Sheffield to Mill River

- **DISTANCE:** 19.0 miles
- **TERRAIN:** Rolling hills; 2 miles of dirt roads
- **DIFFICULTY:** Easy to moderate
- **RECOMMENDED BICYCLE:** Hybrid

This scenic ride passes through spectacular countryside, from dirt roads in quiet woodland to rolling country lanes through pastoral landscapes dotted with barns and stone walls. The tiny hamlet of Mill River, at the ride's halfway point, is the kind of hidden place that makes you feel as if you've stumbled upon a well-kept secret.

Sheffield is a village of firsts. It is Berkshire County's oldest town, settled by Matthew Noble in 1725; the Colonel Ashley House, built in 1735, is the oldest in the Berkshires; and the 1760 Parish Church is the county's oldest church. This much history makes for an interesting kaleidoscope of architecture, from grand Edwardian manor houses to Colonial saltboxes. Many of these historic buildings that line Main Street and the village's quiet back roads have been converted into inns or antiques shops. In fact, Sheffield has the greatest concentration of antiques dealers in Berkshire County.

The Sheffield Congregational Church, built in 1762, towers above the other buildings in the center of the village. The adjacent stone building, a general store, was built of stone from the quarries that once prospered here.

From Sheffield the ride traces rural country roads into Mill River, a village on the Konkapot River. The river is named for Chief Konkapot, who led the Stockbridge Indians when they sold the southern part of Berkshire County to settlers in the 1700s.

As you pedal through this peaceful forest, it might be hard to imagine that many small factories producing paper, textiles, and gunpowder once thrived along the riverbank. Today, the river draws trout fishermen, hikers, and birdwatchers who can explore Umpachene Falls from a trailhead along the road.

DIRECTIONS FOR THE RIDE

The ride begins in Sheffield; start from the parking area along US 7 in front of the Sheffield post office. There are a couple stores here to get food and drinks.

0.0 Leave the parking area and head north on US 7.

0.2 Turn right onto Maple Avenue.

1.0 Turn right onto Hewins Street.
This quiet country road winds through wide open farmland.

4.1 Turn left onto Alum Hill Road.
This hilly road will take you into New Marlborough.

5.4 At the stop sign, turn left onto Clayton Mill River Road.

6.4 Bear left at the Y-junction, following the white signs to Mill River and Mill River General Store.
This quiet scenic road passes some old homesteads before entering the woods and hugging the curves of the Konkapot River. You will pass the dirt road that leads toward the river and Umpachene Falls.

9.2 Just before the village of Mill River, turn right to cross the Konkapot River on a small bridge; then at the stop sign, turn left.
The Mill River General Store is a good stop to pick up provisions and rest on the front porch.

9.7 About 0.5 mile out of the village, bear right onto Hartsville Road.
You will immediately pass New Marlborough Central School.

10.4 Where the pavement ends, bear left at the fork to follow the Konkapot River.

Mill River is a quiet village on the Konkapot River.

The dirt road will follow the river before crossing it on a bridge, then climbing away from the riverbank through the woods.

12.0 Turn left onto Calkins Cross Road.
Look for a tiny unmarked green here flanked by an old farmhouse and barn.

12.4 Turn left onto Mill River–Great Barrington Road (unmarked).
The road becomes paved here once again.

13.4 Bear right onto County Road (unmarked).

18.9 At the stop sign, turn left onto US 7.

19.0 Turn right into the parking area to end the ride.

Bicycle Shops

Berkshire Bike & Blade, 326 Stockbridge Road (US 7), Great Barrington; 413-528-5555

Foster Harland Inc., 15 Bridge Street, Great Barrington; 413-528-0564

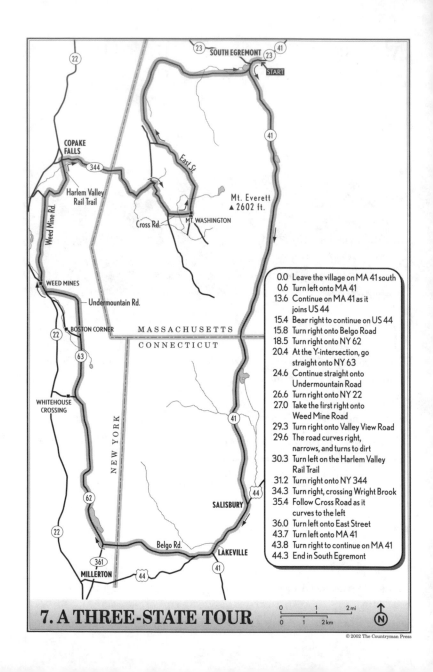

0.0	Leave the village on MA 41 south
0.6	Turn left onto MA 41
13.6	Continue on MA 41 as it joins US 44
15.4	Bear right to continue on US 44
15.8	Turn right onto Belgo Road
18.5	Turn right onto NY 62
20.4	At the Y-intersection, go straight onto NY 63
24.6	Continue straight onto Undermountain Road
26.6	Turn right onto NY 22
27.0	Take the first right onto Weed Mine Road
29.3	Turn right onto Valley View Road
29.6	The road curves right, narrows, and turns to dirt
30.3	Turn left on the Harlem Valley Rail Trail
31.2	Turn right onto NY 344
34.3	Turn right, crossing Wright Brook
35.4	Follow Cross Road as it curves to the left
36.0	Turn left onto East Street
43.7	Turn left onto MA 41
43.8	Turn right to continue on MA 41
44.3	End in South Egremont

7. A THREE-STATE TOUR

© 2002 The Countryman Press

Massachusetts–Connecticut–New York: A Three-State Tour

- **DISTANCE:** 44.3 miles
- **TERRAIN:** Rolling hills with a challenging climb through the Taconic Range
- **DIFFICULTY:** Strenuous
- **RECOMMENDED BICYCLE:** Touring/road bike

This ride explores the rugged hills and rolling farmland where the boundaries of Massachusetts, Connecticut, and New York come together. This remote southwestern corner of Berkshire County is one of the most beautiful—and least visited—parts of the state.

From the Colonial village of South Egremont, you head south through upland farms into Connecticut. All along the way you'll pass many of the homesteads built by the earliest settlers who came to farm these rocky lands.

The northwest corner of Litchfield County contains Connecticut's loftiest peaks, including Bear Mountain, the state's highest summit. The highest point in the state, at 2,380 feet, is on the slopes of Mount Frissell, whose summit is in Massachusetts.

In New York State, you'll ride through rural Dutchess and Columbia Counties. Peaceful country roads roll past farm fields that stretch to the horizon, some filled with rows of corn, others dotted with sheep and cows. High above is the ridgeline of the Taconics and Berkshires, the rugged range that includes the peaks

Bash Bish Falls is a hidden jewel in the Taconic Range.

of Brace, Alander, and Washburn Mountains, rising as high as 2,311 feet.

Part of the route follows the Harlem Valley Rail Trail, a paved bike recreational trail that follows the old New York and Harlem rail line that carried passengers from 1831 until 1972. The bike path will take you into the tiny village of Copake, the last stop before leaving New York over the rugged Taconic Range.

Taconic State Park encompasses more than 5,000 acres spread along an 11-mile border between the three states. The crown jewel of nearby Mount Washington State Forest is Bash Bish Falls, a dramatic waterfall that draws more than 100,000 visitors to this isolated area each year. The brook rushes down a 1,000-foot sheer gorge, then drops over 80 feet to pools below. The falls were painted by Hudson River School artist John F. Kensett several times in the 19th century. A 1-mile hike along Bash Bish Brook climbs through the woods to the towering falls, another leads to the pools at the base. The falls are named for the beautiful Mohican princess Bash Bish who, according to legend, plunged to her death here along with her lover.

Mount Washington is one of the state's least populated villages, with fewer than two hundred year-round residents. Despite the isolation and terrain, Dutch settlers first established a community here in the late 17th century; it was incorporated into a town in 1779. The white clapboard Union Church is open during the summer only. It has the feel of a ghost town, surrounded by more than 5,000 acres of rugged state forest that includes the soaring peak of Mount Everett. At 2,602 feet, its summit is second only to Mount Greylock in the northern Berkshires.

DIRECTIONS FOR THE RIDE
The ride begins at the village green on Main Street (MA 23/41) in South Egremont.

0.0 Leave the village on MA 41 south.

0.6 Turn left onto MA 41.
This rolling road passes beautiful farmland and restored vintage homesteads as you ride south into Connecticut.

13.6 Continue on MA 41 south as it joins US 44 in Salisbury.
Salisbury has a lovely collection of white clapboard homes mixed with boutiques and cafés, popular with well-heeled visitors who retreat to country estates in and around the village.

15.4 Bear right to continue on US 44.
Among the grand estates near Lake Wononskopomuc is the historic Holley-Williams House and Cannon Museum. The 1808 Classical Revival house is full of period artifacts; the museum traces the history of the area's blast furnaces that bustled during the American Revolution and Civil War.

15.8 Turn right onto Belgo Road.
Immediately begin climbing past estates with antique homes and manicured lawns. You will encounter few cars, if any, in these rural foothills of the Taconics on the Connecticut/New York border.

18.5 At the stop sign, turn right at the T-intersection (NY 62).
This is agricultural Dutchess County, a bucolic valley dotted with working farms, estates, and fields stretching along the base of the Taconic Range. This gently rolling valley makes for easy riding as you head north through New York.

20.4 At the unmarked Y-intersection about 1 mile past Rudd Pond, go straight onto NY 63.

24.6 At the sign for Boston Corners Road, continue straight onto Undermountain Road.
Just over the border is a small green sign on a post lodged into a crumbling stone wall. It marks the site of a prize fight held in October 1883, lasting 37 rounds and attended by three thousand people.

26.6 At the stop sign, turn right onto NY 22.

27.0 Take the first right onto Weed Mine Road.

29.3 Turn right at the Y-intersection onto Valley View Road.

29.6 Follow the road as it curves to the right, narrows, and turns to dirt.
Continue as it passes through a farm, although it looks like a private way. The Harlem Valley Rail Trail will shortly join the road.

30.3 Turn left onto the Harlem Valley Rail Trail.
Take the paved path into Copake, a tiny hamlet on the edge of Taconic State Park.

31.2 At the Depot Deli in Copake, turn right onto NY 344, following the sign to Bash Bish Falls.
This is the most challenging leg of the ride. The climb begins gradually, rising along Bash Bish Brook. After the trailhead for the falls, the ascent steepens dramatically, with very narrow and tight turns all the way to the Massachusetts state line at the top of the ridge.

34.3 Turn right, crossing Wright Brook, and follow the sign for Mount Everett Reservation and Salisbury, Connecticut.
Climb away from the brook for the final steep ascent.

35.4 Follow the road as it curves to the left (Cross Road).

36.0 At the stop sign in Mount Washington, turn left onto East Street.
This remote community is little more than a white clapboard church and town hall tucked into the woods. The long descent toward South Egremont will begin on the outskirts of the village.

43.7 At the stop sign, turn left onto MA 41.

43.8 At the next stop sign, turn right to continue on MA 41.

44.3 The ride ends in South Egremont.

Bicycle Shops

Berkshire Bike & Blade, 326 Stockbridge Road (US 7), Great Barrington; 413-528-5555

Foster Harland Inc., 15 Bridge Street, Great Barrington; 413-528-0564

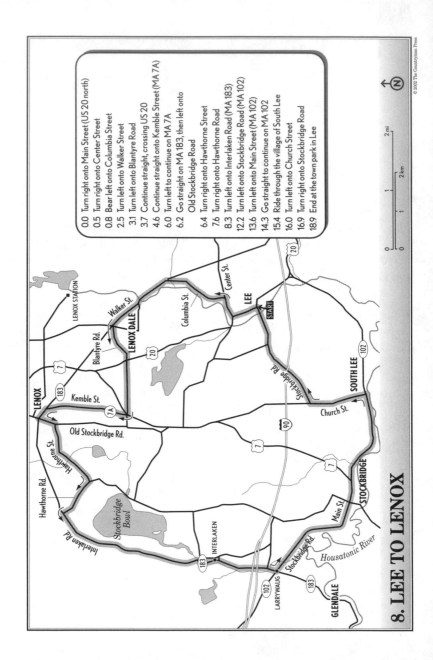

8. LEE TO LENOX

0.0	Turn right onto Main Street (US 20 north)
0.5	Turn right onto Center Street
0.8	Bear left onto Columbia Street
2.5	Turn left onto Walker Street
3.1	Turn left onto Blantyre Road
3.7	Continue straight, crossing US 20
4.6	Continue straight onto Kemble Street (MA 7A)
6.0	Turn left to continue on MA 7A
6.2	Go straight on MA 183, then left onto Old Stockbridge Road
6.4	Turn right onto Hawthorne Street
7.6	Turn right onto Hawthorne Road
8.3	Turn left onto Interlaken Road (MA 183)
12.2	Turn left onto Stockbridge Road (MA 102)
13.6	Turn left onto Main Street (MA 102)
14.3	Go straight to continue on MA 102
15.4	Ride through the village of South Lee
16.0	Turn left onto Church Street
16.9	Turn right onto Stockbridge Road
18.9	End at the town park in Lee

© 2002 The Countryman Press

Lee to Lenox

- **DISTANCE:** 18.9 miles
- **TERRAIN:** Gradual to moderately rolling hills
- **DIFFICULTY:** Easy to moderate
- **RECOMMENDED BICYCLE:** Touring/road bike

The historic town of Lee is a study in contrasts. The buildings crammed along Main Street are a diverse mix of Federal, Victorian, Italianate, and Greek Revival architecture. The First Congregational Church, with its soaring steeple (the tallest wood frame steeple in the country) and trompe-l'oeil work inside, and the Beaux Arts–style library are among the grand buildings on the national historic register. Elegant Victorian houses are open as bed & breakfasts, working farms line upland roads, and paper, marble, and lime are still produced in South Lee.

Lee—named for Revolutionary War general Charles Lee—was famous in the 1800s for papermaking and marble quarrying. Lee marble is in the customhouse in Manhattan, headstones in Arlington National Cemetery, and in the Washington Monument. It's also in the town park, in the drinking fountain designed by renowned sculptor Daniel Chester French, who summered on an estate in nearby Lenox (see Ride 3: Stockbridge).

The Hurlbut Mill in South Lee is a homage to the town's indus-trial history. Papermaking became a pioneering industry in the Berkshires when Samuel Church built the first paper mill on the

The historic Hurlbut paper mill on the banks of the Housatonic River

Housatonic River in the early 19th century. In 1882 Thomas Hurlbut started producing paper here; 50 years later his sons built the massive, five-story brick mill that now houses the paper-making giant Mead Corporation.

Lenox was incorporated in 1767 and named for Charles Lenox, the Duke of Richmond. It was the county seat from 1787 until it moved to Pittsfield in 1868. This is one of the most gentrified villages in the Berkshires, full of gracious 19th-century buildings like the Federal-style courthouse, and the handsome Church on the Hill.

The late-19th-century elite, drawn by the climate and scenery, built baronial mansions and made this their summer playground, earning Lenox the name inland Newport. Edith Wharton's estate, The Mount—modeled after Christopher Wren's Belton House in Lincolnshire—is now home to Shakespeare & Co., one of North America's largest Shakespeare festivals. Scenes from her novel *Ethan Frome* were set around the village. Her Mediterranean-style villa, surrounded by piazzas and terraced gardens, is open to visitors.

One of the many estate-turned-resorts is Bellefontaine, a white marble and redbrick palatial estate built in 1897 by architects of the New York Public Library for tycoon Giraud Foster. Today it's Canyon Ranch, an exclusive spa where the well-heeled go to unwind.

Stockbridge is one of the most charming villages in the Berkshires; Norman Rockwell's famous painting of Main Street made it synonymous with quintessential New England in the minds of many visitors. Be sure to take in Main Street's well-preserved antique homes, the Mission House, the handsome brick First Congregational Church, the white-columned town hall, and, of course, the Red Lion Inn at the heart of the village.

DIRECTIONS FOR THE RIDE

The ride begins at the town park at the south end of Main Street in downtown Lee. There is parking around the green on Park Place or in a municipal parking lot on Railroad Street (off Main Street).

0.0 From the town park, turn right onto Main Street (US 20 north).
Downtown Lee is crammed with shops and cafés in buildings with an eclectic mix of architecture.

0.5 At the top of Main Street, turn right onto Center Street (US 20 makes a sharp left turn here).

0.8 Bear left onto Columbia Street, following the Housatonic River.

2.5 At the stop sign in Lenox Dale, turn left onto Walker Street.
The road passes a few shops, then curves to the right and climbs toward Lenox.

3.1 At the top of the hill, turn left onto Blantyre Road.
Blantyre is an exclusive resort in a 1902 Tudor-style mansion styled after a baronial Scottish manor house; it's under the same ownership as the Red Lion Inn in Stockbridge.

3.7 Continue straight at the stop sign, crossing US 20.
Cranwell Resort & Golf Club is a 380-acre hilltop resort, a former 1890s summer estate.

4.6 At the traffic light, cross US 7 and continue straight onto Kemble Street (MA 7A).
Bellefontaine—now Canyon Ranch—was one of the grandest summer "cottages" in Lenox, built in the 1890s to replicate Louis XVI's Petit Trianon. Edith Wharton's estate (The Mount) and Shakespeare & Co. are also in the neighborhood.

6.0 At the stop sign, turn left to continue on MA 7A.
Elegant inns and boutiques line this street that leads into the center of the village.

6.2 At the four-way intersection in the center of town, go straight on MA 183, then immediately left onto Old Stockbridge Road (next to the Lenox police department).

6.4 Turn right onto Hawthorne Street.

7.6 At the stop sign, turn right onto Hawthorne Road.
The tidy red farmhouse sitting high above Stockbridge Bowl on Hawthorne Road is a reproduction of the summer home that novelist Nathaniel Hawthorne lived in with his family. The original burned down in the 1890s; the painstaking reproduction was completed based on photographs.

8.3 At the stop sign, turn left onto Interlaken Road (MA 183).
Gould Meadows slopes along the road and into the forest; there are stunning views of the Berkshire Hills and Stockbridge Bowl on the descent toward Tanglewood, summer home of the Boston Symphony Orchestra since the 1930s.

11.0 Pass by the village of Interlaken.

12.2 At the blinking traffic light, turn left onto Stockbridge Road (MA 102).
This long, flat rural stretch of road will bring you into the outlying neighborhoods of Stockbridge. Also here is the Berkshire Botanical Garden, a 15-acre botanical museum with more than 2,500 varieties of plants. Visitors can tour herb, vegetable, rose, and other specialty gardens.

13.6 At the stop sign, turn left onto Main Street (MA 102).

14.0 Pass through the village of Stockbridge.
Use caution in this very busy area.

14.3 Where US 7 turns left, go straight to continue on MA 102.

15.4 Ride through the village of South Lee.

The Merrell Tavern Inn is a stately redbrick home with double white-columned porches that was built in 1794 as a stagecoach stop. The Federal House Inn is a handsome 1824 pillared home built by Thomas Hurlbut so he could be close to his paper mills. The home stayed in the Hurlbut family for more than 125 years.

16.0 Turn left onto Church Street.
There is a moderate climb here for nearly 1 mile.

16.9 At the stop sign, turn right onto Stockbridge Road.
This back road rolls up and down short hills before descending into Lee.

18.9 The ride ends at the town park in Lee.

Bicycle Shops

The Arcadian Shop, 91 Pittsfield Road (US 7), Lenox; 1-800-239-3391

Main Street Sports & Leisure, 48 Main Street (MA 7A), Lenox; 413-637-4407

Mean Wheels Bike Shop, 57A Housatonic Street, Lenox; 413-637-0644

THE
NORTHERN
BERKSHIRES

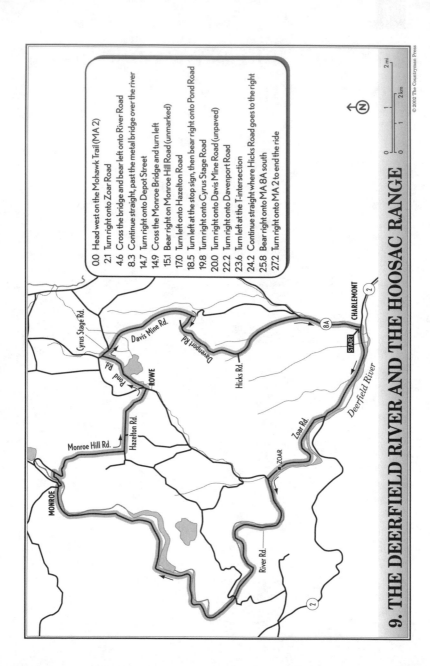

9. THE DEERFIELD RIVER AND THE HOOSAC RANGE

0.0 Head west on the Mohawk Trail (MA 2)
2.1 Turn right onto Zoar Road
4.6 Cross the bridge and bear left onto River Road
8.3 Continue straight, past the metal bridge over the river
14.7 Turn right onto Depot Street
14.9 Cross the Monroe Bridge and turn left
15.1 Bear right on Monroe Hill Road (unmarked)
17.0 Turn left onto Hazelton Road
18.5 Turn left at the stop sign, then bear right onto Pond Road
19.8 Turn right onto Cyrus Stage Road
20.0 Turn right onto Davis Mine Road (unpaved)
22.2 Turn right onto Davenport Road
23.6 Turn left at the T-intersection
24.2 Continue straight where Hicks Road goes to the right
25.8 Bear right onto MA 8A south
27.2 Turn right onto MA 2 to end the ride

© 2002 The Countryman Press

9

The Deerfield River and the Hoosac Range

- ■ **DISTANCE:** 27.2 miles
- ■ **TERRAIN:** Rolling hills with a steep climb above the Deerfield River
- ■ **DIFFICULTY:** Strenuous
- ■ **RECOMMENDED BICYCLE:** Hybrid

This ride passes through some of the most rugged terrain in the northern Berkshires, a very beautiful yet largely overlooked area compared with most of the county. In autumn, thousands drive along the Mohawk Trail to witness the rich pageant of autumn foliage, but relatively few tourists venture onto the web of nearby back roads that follow the Deerfield River and spread across thousands of acres of state forest that blanket the ridges of the Hoosac Range.

It leaves those who are willing to explore it richly rewarded. This is wooded, rugged backcountry, with scattered old farms that were built in the Deerfield River's fertile floodplain in the 1700s. The river flows through from Vermont on its way southeast to its confluence with the Connecticut River.

Charlemont was settled in 1749 and sits on the Mohawk Trail, the 38-mile tourist route that follows an old Native American foot-path through this northernmost part of Hampshire and Berkshire Counties. Anglers and white-water enthusiasts flock to the river from spring to fall, skiers come to the slopes of Berkshire East Ski

Area in winter, and audiences gather every summer in the Charlemont Federated Church to hear classical chamber music. Regardless, the back roads remain quiet. As you follow the river north, you'll pass the eastern portal of the Hoosac Tunnel, built in the late 1800s to connect the land west of this impenetrable mountain range to Boston and eastern Massachusetts. The tunnel was blasted through miles of solid granite, costing $15 million and two hundred lives.

Rowe is a tiny backcountry village of fewer than four hundred residents, perched high on a hill surrounded by fields and heavily wooded hills. New England's first atomic energy plant, which operated here in the early 1960s, looms over the river at Monroe Bridge. In the late 19th and early 20th century, this area boomed with industry, including a tool factory, casket shop, and several mills. Today it's peaceful and remote; the only hints of the past are in the Rowe Historical Society Museum and on the small plaques around town where the factories once stood.

DIRECTIONS FOR THE RIDE

The ride begins in the center of Charlemont. There are parking areas along the Mohawk Trail (MA 2) and a couple general stores in the village to pick up food and drinks.

0.0 Head west out of Charlemont on the Mohawk Trail (MA 2).

2.1 Turn right onto Zoar Road.
Turn just before the bridge, following the small brown sign for Zoar Road.

4.6 Cross the bridge and bear left onto River Road.
The road narrows as it passes under railroad tracks and follows the riverbank.

5.4 Pass by the Zoar Picnic Area.
These picnic sites in a pine grove by the river make a good rest stop. Farther along the road, near the junction of Whitcomb Summit Road, is the eastern portal of the Hoosac Tunnel.

8.3 At the green sign for Monroe and Bear Swamp, continue straight, past the metal bridge over the river.
The road will begin climbing into the hills above the river. You'll also pass the Bear Swamp Generating Station and Fife Brook Dam.

14.7 Turn right onto Depot Street in Monroe Bridge.
This small village of modest homes clustered along the river sits below the decommissioned Yankee Rowe Nuclear Power Plant.

14.9 Cross the Monroe Bridge, turn left, and climb to the Y-intersection at the Yankee Visitors Center.

15.1 Bear right on Monroe Hill Road (unmarked), a very strenuous climb that winds up the mountain for about 1 mile before descending through Monroe State Forest.

17.0 At the T-intersection, turn left onto Hazleton Road.

18.5 Turn left at the stop sign, then bear immediately right onto Pond Road.
Look for a white sign for Whitingham and Heath, and the white clapboard Rowe town hall across the street.

19.8 Turn right onto Cyrus Stage Road, at the white sign for the town of Heath.

The Deerfield River near Charlemont

20.0 Take the first right onto Davis Mine Road (unpaved).
You'll pass a swamp, then climb and descend through forested hills. Pelham Lake Park Game Sanctuary protects 1,000 acres on the lakeshore, where Fort Pelham stood in the 18th century.

22.2 Turn right onto Davenport Road.

22.6 Bear left as the road curves right; look for the Davenport trailhead straight ahead.

23.6 At the T-intersection, turn left (see a sign for Tatro Road to the right). *Use caution in this remote area; the descent gets steeper, and the road is rough in places.*

24.2 Continue straight where Hicks Road goes to the right.

25.2 The pavement returns at Maxwell Road (unmarked).

25.8 Bear right onto MA 8A south.
Follow the road downhill to return to Charlemont.

27.2 At the stop sign in Charlemont, turn right onto MA 2 to end the ride.

Bicycle Shops

Berkshire Outfitters, MA 8, Adams; 413-743-5900

The Sports Corner, 61 Main Street, North Adams; 413-664-8654

10

The Northern Berkshires

- ■ **DISTANCE:** 54.8 miles
- ■ **TERRAIN:** Gradual to steep hills connected by rolling terrain
- ■ **DIFFICULTY:** Strenuous
- ■ **RECOMMENDED BICYCLE:** Touring/road bike

This ride has its share of arduous climbing but ends on fairly gentle terrain, thanks to the Hoosic and Housatonic Rivers, which flow through the northern Berkshires.

You'll begin in North Adams, a historic 19th-century mill city. Sprawling mill buildings and warehouses front the Hoosic River, harking to the city's heyday when it was a bustling industrial hub, producing machinery, textiles, fabrics, and leather goods.

In the 1970s, when many of the mills left New England for the South, North Adams slipped rapidly into economic decline. Today an earnest revitalization is under way, and the city now boasts unique cultural attractions and historic sites that lure thousands of visitors each year. The Massachusetts Museum of Contemporary Art (MASS MoCA) is the nation's largest contemporary art museum, featuring minimalist and conceptual art, as well as film and video exhibits and concerts. The city's proud industrial heritage is on display at Western Gateway Heritage State Park, which illustrates the history of the city's industrial and railroad past, especially the famed Hoosac Tunnel. Engineers used nitroglycerine—an innovative method for the 1800s—to blast through 5 miles of solid

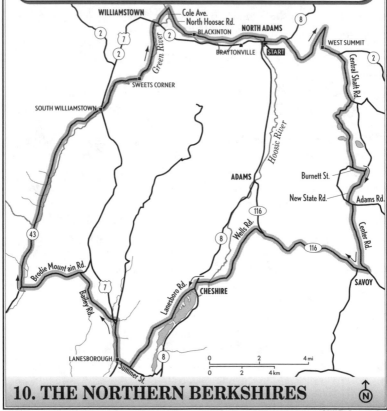

0.0	Turn left onto Holden Street
0.1	Turn right onto River Street
0.3	Cross Eagle Street at the light
0.4	Turn left on MA 2/MA 8
1.0	Bear right onto MA 2
3.8	Follow the hairpin turn to the right
4.8	Cross over West Summit
5.4	Turn right onto Central Shaft Road
5.8	Bear right and follow signs to Savoy Mountain State Forest
7.4	Turn right
8.7	Stay on the paved road as it bears left
10.7	Follow to left as road becomes Burnett Road (unmarked)
11.1	Bear right onto New State Road (unmarked)
12.6	Turn left onto Adams Road (unmarked)
12.8	Bear right onto paved Center Road
15.7	Turn right onto MA 116/8A
16.2	Stay on MA 116 as MA 8A goes left
20.6	Cross a bridge, turn left onto Wells Road
24.1	Bear right onto Church Street
24.5	Turn left onto MA 8
24.8	Turn right onto Lanesboro Road
29.0	Turn right onto Summer Street (unmarked)
29.6	Turn right onto US 7
31.2	Turn left onto Bailey Road
33.7	Turn left onto Brodie Mountain Road
36.2	Turn right onto MA 43
44.4	Cross US 7 to continue on MA 43 (Green River Road)
49.2	Turn right onto MA 2 (Main Street)
49.3	Turn left onto Cole Avenue
50.0	Turn right onto North Hoosac Road
53.0	Bear left at the Y-intersection
54.6	Turn right onto Holden Street
54.8	Turn right onto St. Anthony's Drive to end

10. THE NORTHERN BERKSHIRES

© 2002 The Countryman Press

granite beneath the Hoosac Range. It cost $15 million and two hundred lives, earning it the unfortunate nickname the Bloody Pit, but provided the first rail connection through the Berkshires from Boston.

You'll climb into the Hoosac Range east of North Adams on the Mohawk Trail, a 38-mile stretch of MA 2 from the New York border to the Connecticut River Valley. It opened in 1914 and became a popular tourist route that follows the old trail between the Hudson and Connecticut River Valleys used by Mohawk Indians during the French and Indian War. There are dramatic mountain vistas along the way, especially around the hairpin turn at West Summit.

Savoy Mountain State Forest comprises 11,118 acres of heavily forested hills. A Shaker community settled here in the early 1800s; today only cellar holes remain. North Pond is popular with anglers; trailheads for the state forest's 24 miles of trails line the roads.

The ride passes through the small village of Cheshire, then follows the shoreline of the 4-mile-long Cheshire Reservoir. You will cross below the mountain range that includes Mount Greylock, the state's highest peak, which towers above the northern Berkshires, then head northwest to the village of Williamstown.

This classic New England town in the state's northwestern corner is surrounded by miles of rural farmland. The village and Williams College are named for Colonel Ephraim Williams Jr., one of the original settlers who died in the French and Indian War and bequeathed his estate to build a college in what was then West Hoosuck. Campus buildings boast a variety of architecture spanning from the 1790s, and the college is one of the most highly regarded small liberal arts institutions in the country.

DIRECTIONS FOR THE RIDE

The ride begins in North Adams near the Massachusetts Museum of Contemporary Art (MASS MoCA). Park in the metered parking lot in front of the museum and the redbrick St. Anthony's parish building at Holden Street.

0.0 Leave the parking lot facing the shopping center onto St. Anthony's Drive and turn left onto Holden Street.

0.1 At the stop sign, turn right onto River Street.
Use caution riding on this busy street.

0.3 At the traffic light, go straight, crossing Eagle Street. This will turn into Canal Street.

0.4 At the stop sign, turn left onto MA 2/MA 8.
Gradually climb away from the brick factory buildings on the outskirts of North Adams.

1.0 Bear right onto MA 2, heading east where MA 8 continues north toward Clarksburg.

3.8 Follow the hairpin turn to the right.
As the climb steepens the views open into the valley and toward the massive hulk of Mount Greylock in the distance. You'll see the many spires reaching out of the valley that give North Adams the nickname the Spire City.

4.8 Cross over West Summit.
The summit is the highest point on the Mohawk Trail and has a 100-mile view into four states.

5.4 Turn right onto Central Shaft Road at the brown sign for Savoy Mountain State Forest.

5.8 Bear right to continue following signs to Savoy Mountain State Forest.

7.4 Turn right and follow the next state forest sign.

8.7 Stay on the paved road as it bears left at a boat launch.
You can catch glimpses of North Pond through the trees. There once was a private resort on this quiet lakeshore. A short section of rough pavement soon makes way to a dirt surface at the Savoy town line.

10.7 Follow the road to the left as it turns into Burnett Road (unmarked) and descends through the woods.

11.1 Pass a parking lot on the left, then bear right onto New State Road (unmarked).
Immediately cross a bridge over Gulf Brook.

12.6 At the T-intersection, turn left onto Adams Road (unmarked).

12.8 Bear right onto paved Center Road; look for the rusted sign pointing to Savoy and MA 116.
Savoy Center consists of little more than a modest brick house and a cluster of headstones across the street.

15.7 At the stop sign, turn right onto MA 116/8A.

16.2 Stay on MA 116 as MA 8A goes left.
A short climb is followed by a long descent with sharp curves. Mount Greylock is directly ahead.

20.6 Cross a bridge over a brook, then turn left onto Wells Road.

24.1 Bear right on Church Street and pass through Cheshire.
This community of dairy farms was made famous by cheese. In 1801, local farmers sent a 1,235-pound block of cheese to Washington, D.C. as a gift to President Thomas Jefferson. A monument to Cheshire cheese stands in the center of the village.

24.5 At the traffic light, turn left onto MA 8.
There is a convenience store here for food and supplies.

24.8 Take the first right onto Lanesboro Road.
You'll follow the reservoir, then climb above it over rolling pastoral hills with long views.

29.0 At the stop sign, turn right onto Summer Street (unmarked), following the sign for US 7.

29.6 Turn right onto US 7.

31.2 Turn left onto Bailey Road, just past the entrance to the Mount Greylock State Reservation.
After climbing through wooded hills, there are open views at a hilltop farm.

33.7 At the stop sign, turn left onto Brodie Mountain Road.
After a short climb, begin a long descent into the village of Hancock.

36.2 At the traffic light, turn right onto MA 43.
This long valley leads north to Williamstown.

44.4 At the stop sign and blinking red light, cross US 7 in South Williamstown to continue on MA 43 (Green River Road).
The historic Store at Five Corners has groceries and a deli.

49.2 At the stop sign in Williamstown, turn right onto MA 2 (Main Street).
This charming New England village is centered on the sprawling campus of Williams College.

49.3 At the traffic light, turn left onto Cole Avenue.

50.0 Cross two bridges—first over a river, then over railroad tracks—and turn right onto North Hoosac Road.

53.0 Bear left at the Y-intersection.

54.6 Turn right onto Holden Street at The Corner Market variety store.

54.8 Turn right onto St. Anthony's Drive, then left into the parking lot to end the ride.

Bicycle Shops

The Sports Corner, 61 Main Street, North Adams; 413-664-8654

Mountain Goat Bicycle Shop, 130 Water Street, Williamstown; 413-458-8445

The Spoke, 279 Main Street (MA 2), Williamstown; 413-458-3456

11

Williamstown

- **DISTANCE:** 12.8 miles
- **TERRAIN:** Low hills; a couple short dirt roads
- **DIFFICULTY:** Easy
- **RECOMMENDED BICYCLE:** Hybrid

Williamstown was established in 1753 by soldiers from Fort Massachusetts who named the outpost settlement West Hoosuck. This classic New England village is the northernmost in the Berkshires, just as it was in the early days of the Massachusetts Bay Colony. One of the soldiers was Colonel Ephraim Williams Jr., who was killed in the French and Indian War in 1755. In his will, he bequeathed his estate to establish a college with the stipulation that the town be named after him.

Today, Williams College is regarded as one of the nation's best small liberal arts institutions. It was a men's college from the 18th century until women were admitted in 1970. During the academic year, the college sponsors a full schedule of concerts, performances, lectures, and exhibitions on campus. The Williamstown Theatre Festival, held each summer, is among the best in the country. Williams College Museum of Art on Lawrence Hall Drive is one of the nation's finest college art museums. More than 11,000 works represent a variety of periods and cultures. Another gem is the Clark Art Institute, founded by art collectors Sterling and Francine Clark. The world-class collection features mostly late-19th-century

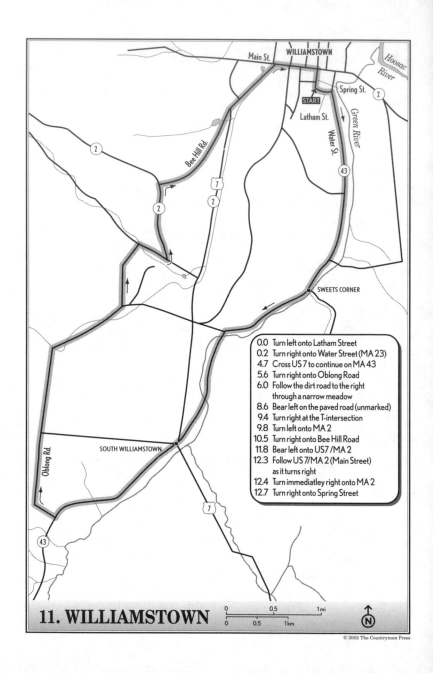

Main St. **WILLIAMSTOWN** Hoosac River

START

Spring St.

Latham St.

Bee Hill Rd.

Water St.

Green River

SWEETS CORNER

Oblong Rd.

SOUTH WILLIAMSTOWN

0.0	Turn left onto Latham Street
0.2	Turn right onto Water Street (MA 23)
4.7	Cross US 7 to continue on MA 43
5.6	Turn right onto Oblong Road
6.0	Follow the dirt road to the right through a narrow meadow
8.6	Bear left on the paved road (unmarked)
9.4	Turn right at the T-intersection
9.8	Turn left onto MA 2
10.5	Turn right onto Bee Hill Road
11.8	Bear left onto US 7 / MA 2
12.3	Follow US 7/MA 2 (Main Street) as it turns right
12.4	Turn immediatley right onto MA 2
12.7	Turn right onto Spring Street

11. WILLIAMSTOWN

0   0.5   1 mi
0   0.5   1 km

N

© 2002 The Countryman Press

French impressionist paintings, including works by Monet, Goya, and Degas. There are more than 30 Renoirs, plus well-known American period pieces, medieval paintings, and other works.

The ride follows the twisting Green River into the bucolic countryside of South Williamstown. On hidden back roads you'll pass gentrified farms and sprawling estates surrounded by meadows and wooded hills.

DIRECTIONS FOR THE RIDE
The ride begins at the public parking lot at the end of Spring Street in the center of Williamstown.

0.0 Leave the parking area by turning left onto Latham Street.

0.2 At the stop sign, turn right onto Water Street (MA 43).
You will ride through an area of historic homes, shops, and cafés that quickly gives way to a flat winding country road hugging the Green River.

4.7 At the stop sign in South Williamstown, go straight across US 7 to continue on MA 43.
The 1770 Store at Five Corners, a landmark at this rural crossroads, is a general store with a deli.

5.6 Turn right onto Oblong Road.
This road rolls through gentle hills with pleasant mountain views.

6.0 Follow the dirt road to the right through a narrow meadow, heading first straight toward the hills, and then curving right to parallel them.

8.6 Bear left on the paved road (unmarked), following the sign to Mount Carmel.

9.4 After descending a short hill, turn right at the T-intersection.
Cross the stone bridge over the stream and continue riding through the woods.

9.8 At the stop sign, turn left onto MA 2. OPTION: Turn right onto MA 2 for a shorter loop that avoids a descent on a dirt road.
Immediately begin a steep but short climb.

10.5 Take the first right onto Bee Hill Road.
Use caution as you descend this steep dirt road. It will be difficult to ignore the striking views into the valley below.

The northern Berkshires are laced with rural backroads.

11.8 Bear left onto US 7/MA 2, following the road back into Williamstown.

12.3 Follow US 7/MA 2 (Main Street) as it turns right.

12.4 Turn immediately right onto MA 2 (US 7 will continue north here). *You will be back at the Williams College campus.*

12.7 Turn right onto Spring Street.

12.8 The ride ends in the parking lot at the end of Spring Street.

Bicycle Shops

Mountain Goat Bicycle Shop, 130 Water Street, Williamstown; 413-458-8445

The Spoke, 279 Main Street (MA 2), Williamstown; 413-458-3456

Mount Greylock

- **DISTANCE:** 35.4 miles
- **TERRAIN:** Very steep, twisting roads to the summit; rolling terrain on the rest of the route
- **DIFFICULTY:** Strenuous
- **RECOMMENDED BICYCLE:** Touring/road bike

Conquering the state's highest summit has been popular for centuries. Yale University president Timothy Dwight wrote a popular guidebook on the mountain in 1800. Many artists and writers have been inspired by Mount Greylock's views, among them Nathaniel Hawthorne, Herman Melville, and Henry David Thoreau, who hiked to the top and penned essays raving of the experience and the lofty heights. Melville could see the mountain from his Arrowhead estate in Pittsfield and is said to have been inspired by its resemblance to a great whale when he wrote *Moby-Dick*.

Today the paved road to the top makes for an easy journey by car. By bicycle, the 8-mile climb to the 3,491-foot peak is arduous but far more rewarding.

The Mount Greylock State Reservation, the state's oldest, protects 12,500 acres of wooded slopes and hills that spread into six towns. It contains New England's only known stands of old-growth red spruce—a 153-acre site on the steep northwest slopes of the mountain—as well as the only subalpine environment in the state. Mount Greylock and the state's second and third highest peaks are in a range that collectively divides the area's two major north-south arteries: US 7 on the west and MA 8 on the east.

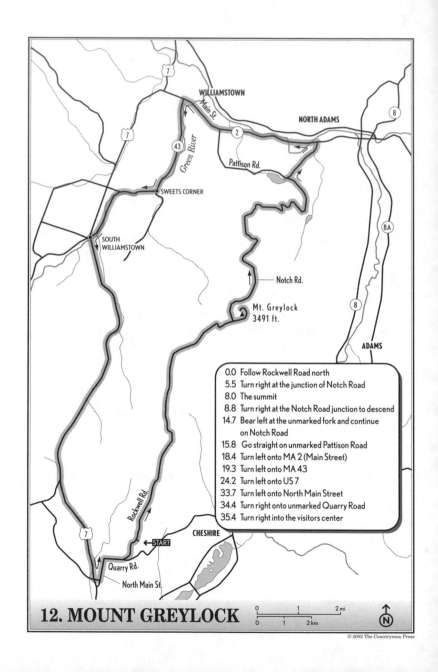

0.0 Follow Rockwell Road north
5.5 Turn right at the junction of Notch Road
8.0 The summit
8.8 Turn right at the Notch Road junction to descend
14.7 Bear left at the unmarked fork and continue on Notch Road
15.8 Go straight on unmarked Pattison Road
18.4 Turn left onto MA 2 (Main Street)
19.3 Turn left onto MA 43
24.2 Turn left onto US 7
33.7 Turn left onto North Main Street
34.4 Turn right onto unmarked Quarry Road
35.4 Turn right into the visitors center

12. MOUNT GREYLOCK

0   1   2 mi
0   1   2 km

N

© 2002 The Countryman Press

The mountain is named for Chief Gray-lock, leader of the local Waranoak Indians who inhabited the Connecticut River Valley in the 17th and 18th centuries. Native Americans believed the mountain was sacred, and according to legend, the chief lived in secret caves on the steep slopes.

Colonel Ephraim Williams Jr. began farming the foot of the mountain in 1739, calling it Grand Hoosuc. In the early 19th century it was known as Saddleback Mountain because of its outline from the south. Saddle Ball Mountain is the peak nearest the summit; depending on your vantage point, it can look higher than Mount Greylock.

Jeremiah Wilbur began farming on the slopes in 1767 and built the first carting roads, including one that approached the summit and is now Notch Road. He cleared the slopes to grow hay and graze herds of cattle and built cider mills, gristmills, and sawmills on Notch Brook.

In the 1800s, North Adams and Adams were booming in the Industrial Revolution, and natural resources, primarily timber, were needed to power the mills and factories at the foot of the mountain. After much of the east face was stripped of first-growth timber, conservation-minded residents stepped in. They purchased 400 acres on the summit and rallied for state protection, which was granted by the end of the century.

Those that reach the summit will be rewarded on clear days with a panoramic view stretching 100 miles into six states. Open pasture, farms, woodland, and the mill town of North Adams fill the Berkshire Valley. The Adirondacks, Catskills, and Green Mountains make a dramatic background. Above, hawks ride the air currents, and hikers cross the mountain on the Appalachian Trail.

Bascom Lodge is a rustic fieldstone building at the summit, built by the Civilian Conservation Corps in 1937 and maintained by the Appalachian Mountain Club. Spending the night here is a unique experience: This is the only mountain in New England that has a lodge at the summit. From summer to fall, private double rooms and large bunk rooms are available, and meals are also served. For information about staying at the lodge, call 413-743-1591.

This is a challenging ride, but imagine tackling the summit as part of a century ride. The Berkshire Cycling Association, a local bicycle racing club, sponsors the Mount Greylock Bicycle Century each summer. The 100-mile route involves 7,000 feet of climbing through the northern Berkshires and Pioneer Valley, including the grueling climb over Mount Greylock. The annual Mount Greylock Ramble, a group climb to the summit, is held on Columbus Day weekend.

The road through the reservation to the summit is generally open from mid-May through mid-October, depending on the weather. Road construction is slated for the next two years; it is wise to call ahead before planning this ride. The phone number for the visitors center is 413-499-4262.

DIRECTIONS FOR THE RIDE

Start the ride at the Mount Greylock Visitors Center at the southern tip of the reservation on Rockwell Road, between US 7 and MA 8 in Lanesborough.

0.0 From the visitors center, follow Rockwell Road as it climbs north toward the summit.
The route is crisscrossed with trails, including the venerable Appalachian Trail, which passes over the lofty summit. The most difficult sections of climbing are the first mile and the last 3 miles before reaching the top; in between is a combination of moderate hills and descents.

5.5 At the junction of Notch Road, turn right to go to the summit.
The first panoramic views can be seen here through the thick woods. Use caution on the switchbacks.

8.0 The summit is marked by Bascom Lodge and the soaring Summit Veterans Memorial Tower.
The 92-foot-high stone tower was built in the 1930s as the state's official war memorial. From it you can look down on the nearby peaks of Mount Prospect, Saddle Ball Mountain, Mount Williams, and Mount Fitch. After visiting the summit, begin the descent by returning down the same road.

8.8 Back at the Notch Road junction, turn right and begin the steep and twisting descent on the mountain's north side.

The Summit Veterans Memorial Tower sits on the highest point in Massachusetts.

14.7 Just after leaving the reservation, bear left at the unmarked fork and continue on Notch Road.

15.8 At the T-intersection, go straight on unmarked Pattison Road, passing by a reservoir.

18.4 At the stop sign, turn left onto MA 2 (Main Street).
This busy commercial area includes several convenience stores and delis, as well as a bike shop.

19.3 Turn left onto MA 43 at the edge of the Williams College campus in Williamstown.

24.2 At the blinking traffic light in South Williamstown, turn left onto US 7.
The historic Store at Five Corners has a deli.

33.7 Turn left onto North Main Street, just past the sign for the Mount Greylock State Reservation.
The road here climbs past a horse farm.

34.4 Turn right onto unmarked Quarry Road, following the brown reservation sign.

35.4 Turn right into the visitors center to end the ride.

Bicycle Shops

Berkshire Outfitters, MA 8, Adams; 413-743-5900

The Sports Corner, 61 Main Street, North Adams; 413-664-8654

The Spoke, 279 Main Street (MA 2), Williamstown; 413-458-3456

13

The Berkshire Hills:
A Two-Day Tour

- **DISTANCE:** 117.2 miles total; 55.5 miles (Day One) and 61.7 miles (Day Two)
- **TERRAIN:** Gradual to steep hills connected by rolling terrain
- **DIFFICULTY:** Strenuous
- **RECOMMENDED BICYCLE:** Touring/road bike

This two-day tour through western Massachusetts—from Great Barrington in the southern Berkshires to Williamstown in the county's northern reaches—is a study in contrasts. It starts in rolling countryside near the New York state line and passes through a string of Colonial villages, some with galleries and trendy boutiques, others looking much as they did two hundred years ago. You'll ride through a landscape of open farmland in the Housatonic River Valley, punctuated by the long, rather low ridges of the Berkshire Hills. The second day starts in a classic New England college town; tours the historic mill towns of North Adams, Adams, and Dalton; climbs Washington Mountain in October Mountain State Forest; and visits a string of Berkshire villages.

A highlight of the first day is the preserved Hancock Shaker Village in Pittsfield. It was founded in 1790 as a self-supporting community whose ideals of simplicity and practicality are evident in their architecture and famous inventions, from packaged seeds and the circular saw to the flat broom and clothespins.

In the 1840s, this was the country's most successful communitarian society. At its peak there were six thousand members, and it remained active until 1960. Today the village is a museum, with demonstrations in furniture making, cooking, farming, music, and craftsmanship. Twenty restored buildings, a farm, and gardens show the Shaker way of life.

The first day ends in the Colonial village of Williamstown. Williams College has the quintessential New England college campus: Gracious brick buildings spread around a historic village, two world-renown art museums, and an esteemed summer drama festival. The community's name changed from West Hoosac to Williamstown when Colonel Ephraim Williams Jr. endowed a college. It was founded in 1791 and today sits high among the country's elite small colleges. The Sterling and Francine Clark Art Institute and the Williams College Museum of Art are top-notch facilities. The Williamstown Theatre Festival features top actors and actresses each summer. The college supports an interesting mix of shops, cafés, and charming inns, making it a good place to stay overnight.

The mill city of North Adams, with roots deep in industry, stands in stark contrast to the genteel air of Williamstown. The sprawling brick mill complexes along the river boomed in the 19th century, producing textiles, leather goods, and tools. Its location at the confluence of the north and south branches of the Hoosic River was ideal for the mills that relied on waterpower.

Like many mill towns, North Adams's vitality was hurt by progress and the exodus of industry from New England. But in 1999 an earnest revitalization included the opening of the Massachusetts Museum of Contemporary Art (MASS MoCA), an art museum and performance center housed in a complex of nearly 30 buildings. In a restored railroad freight yard, Western Gateway Heritage State Park tells the story of the Hoosac Tunnel, the 19th-century railroad tunnel that linked Boston to western Massachusetts through the rugged Hoosac Range.

Adams began as a farming community but turned into a factory town, famous for the textile mills that boomed in the 1800s and brought wealth to many of its residents. A downtown statue of

President William McKinley honors the president who backed a tariff protecting the town's textile industry from foreign competition. Mount Greylock towers over this industrial town, which is also the birthplace of suffragette Susan B. Anthony, who is honored every summer in the Susan B. Anthony Days Festival.

The Crane Museum of Papermaking in Dalton is housed in Crane & Company's 1844 stone mill on the banks of the Housatonic River. Zenas Crane made papers for currency, stock certificates, and stationery in Dalton in the 1800s; his father sold currency paper in 1775 to patriot Paul Revere, who produced the money that helped finance the Revolution. Notice the formidable brick and stone factories and mill buildings along the river.

From Dalton the tour heads south through the state's largest forest and the historic villages of Lee, Stockbridge, and Housatonic before returning to Great Barrington.

DAY ONE

DISTANCE: 55.5 miles

TERRAIN: Rolling hills with a couple steep climbs

ACCOMMODATIONS NEAR THE START OF THE RIDE:

Windflower, 684 South Egremont Road (MA 23), Great Barrington; 1-800-992-1993

Turning Point Inn, corner of MA 23 and Lake Buel Road, Great Barrington; 413-528-4777

Wainright Inn, 518 South Main Street (US 7), Great Barrington; 413-528-2062

The tour begins in downtown Great Barrington. There is public parking at the end of Castle Street. For food and supplies, there are convenience stores in Great Barrington, West Stockbridge, Pittsfield, and Lanesborough.

0.0 Leave Great Barrington on US 7 south (Main Street).
This road through downtown is busy with traffic and pedestrians, especially on weekends.

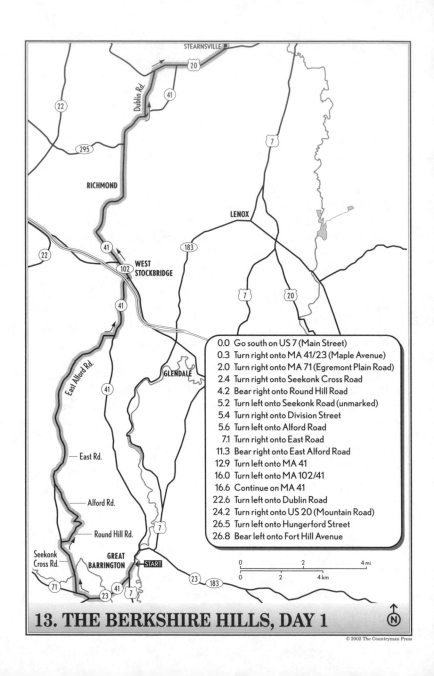

0.0	Go south on US 7 (Main Street)
0.3	Turn right onto MA 41/23 (Maple Avenue)
2.0	Turn right onto MA 71 (Egremont Plain Road)
2.4	Turn right onto Seekonk Cross Road
4.2	Bear right onto Round Hill Road
5.2	Turn left onto Seekonk Road (unmarked)
5.4	Turn right onto Division Street
5.6	Turn left onto Alford Road
7.1	Turn right onto East Road
11.3	Bear right onto East Alford Road
12.9	Turn left onto MA 41
16.0	Turn left onto MA 102/41
16.6	Continue on MA 41
22.6	Turn left onto Dublin Road
24.2	Turn right onto US 20 (Mountain Road)
26.5	Turn left onto Hungerford Street
26.8	Bear left onto Fort Hill Avenue

13. THE BERKSHIRE HILLS, DAY 1

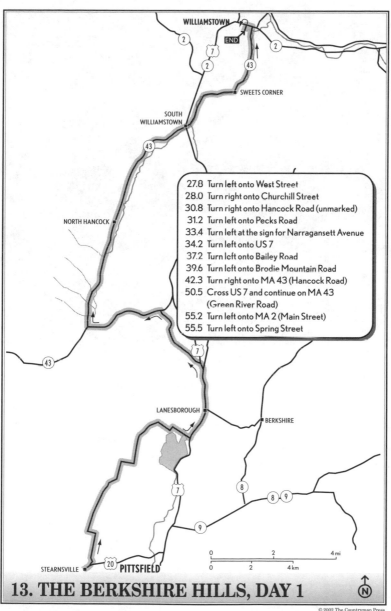

WILLIAMSTOWN

2

7

END

2

43

2

SWEETS CORNER

SOUTH
WILLIAMSTOWN

43

NORTH HANCOCK

27.8 Turn left onto West Street
28.0 Turn right onto Churchill Street
30.8 Turn right onto Hancock Road (unmarked)
31.2 Turn left onto Pecks Road
33.4 Turn left at the sign for Narragansett Avenue
34.2 Turn left onto US 7
37.2 Turn left onto Bailey Road
39.6 Turn left onto Brodie Mountain Road
42.3 Turn right onto MA 43 (Hancock Road)
50.5 Cross US 7 and continue on MA 43
        (Green River Road)
55.2 Turn left onto MA 2 (Main Street)
55.5 Turn left onto Spring Street

7

43

LANESBOROUGH

BERKSHIRE

7

8

8 9

9

STEARNSVILLE   20 PITTSFIELD

0   2   4 mi
0   2   4 km

13. THE BERKSHIRE HILLS, DAY 1

N

© 2002 The Countryman Press

The 1826 Round Stone Barn at Hancock Shaker Village is a fine example of innovative Shaker architecture.

0.3 Turn right onto MA 41/23 (Maple Avenue).
The road curves through an open landscape of farm fields and woodland.

2.0 Turn right onto MA 71 (Egremont Plain Road), following the sign to the airport.

2.4 Turn right onto Seekonk Cross Road.

4.2 Bear right onto Round Hill Road.
This area of working farms is among the most rural in the Berkshires.

5.2 At the stop sign, turn left onto Seekonk Road (unmarked).

5.4 Turn right onto Division Street.

5.6 At the stop sign, turn left onto Alford Road.

7.1 In the village of Alford, turn right onto East Road.
This Colonial village, with its small collection of tidy white clapboard buildings, looks much as it did when it was incorporated in 1750.

11.3 At the Y-intersection, bear right onto East Alford Road.
Use caution on this steep downhill section.

12.9 At the stop sign, turn left onto MA 41.

16.0 At the stop sign, turn left onto MA 102/41 and follow it into West Stockbridge.
The galleries and shops in this lively village make it an interesting place to stop; there is a general store if you need supplies.

16.6 Continue on MA 41 after passing through West Stockbridge.
The Richmond Store, next to the Richmond post office, sells gourmet groceries and artisan cheeses.

22.6 Turn left onto Dublin Road, just past the Richmond Inn.

24.2 At the stop sign, turn right onto US 20 (Mountain Road) and pass Hancock Shaker Village.
Among the preserved buildings visible along the road is the unusual 1826 Round Stone Barn, a testament to the functionality of Shaker architecture and design. It allowed a farmer to single-handedly feed an entire herd of cattle by standing in the center of the barn.

26.5 Turn left onto Hungerford Street, following the sign for Pittsfield State Forest.

26.8 Bear left onto Fort Hill Avenue.

27.8 At the stop sign, turn left onto West Street.

28.0 Take the first right onto Churchill Street.

30.8 Turn right onto Hancock Road (unmarked; look for metal guardrails).

31.2 At the stop sign, turn left onto Pecks Road.

33.4 At the stop sign, turn left at the sign for Narragansett Avenue.
This short, steep descent passes Pontoosuc Lake on the way to US 7.

34.2 At the stop sign, turn left onto US 7.

37.2 Turn left onto Bailey Road.
This road climbs into the forested hills that lead into the northern Berkshires.

39.6 At the stop sign, turn left onto Brodie Mountain Road.
After another 0.5 mile of climbing, the road descends quickly past the slopes of Jiminy Peak Ski Area.

42.3 At the stop sign, turn right onto MA 43 (Hancock Road).

50.5 At the blinking traffic light, cross US 7 in South Williamstown and continue on MA 43 (Green River Road).
The historic Store at Five Corners, established at this rural crossroads in 1770, is a general store with a deli.

55.2 At the stop sign, turn left onto MA 2 (Main Street).

55.5 Turn left onto Spring Street to end the ride in the center of Williamstown.

ACCOMMODATIONS IN THE AREA

The House on Main Street, 1120 Main Street, Williamstown; 413-458-3031

The Orchards, 222 Adams Road (off MA 2), Williamstown; 413-458-9611

Riverbend Farm, 643 Simonds Road (US 7), Williamstown; 413-458-3121

The Williams Inn, Main Street (junction of MA 2 and US 7), Williamstown; 413-458-9371

DAY TWO

DISTANCE: 61.7 miles

TERRAIN: Rolling hills with a steep ascent of Washington Mountain

0.0 From the center of Williamstown, head east on MA 2 (Main Street) and turn left onto Cole Avenue at the traffic light.

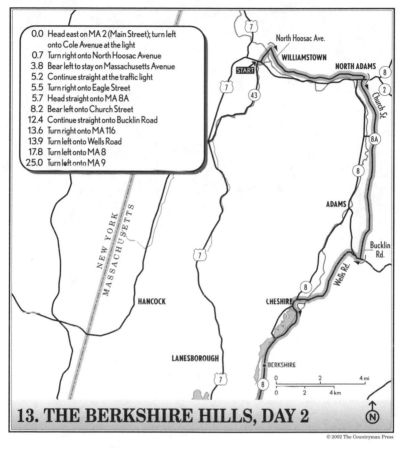

0.0 Head east on MA 2 (Main Street); turn left onto Cole Avenue at the light
0.7 Turn right onto North Hoosac Avenue
3.8 Bear left to stay on Massachusetts Avenue
5.2 Continue straight at the traffic light
5.5 Turn right onto Eagle Street
5.7 Head straight onto MA 8A
8.2 Bear left onto Church Street
12.4 Continue straight onto Bucklin Road
13.6 Turn right onto MA 116
13.9 Turn left onto Wells Road
17.8 Turn left onto MA 8
25.0 Turn left onto MA 9

13. THE BERKSHIRE HILLS, DAY 2

© 2002 The Countryman Press

0.7 Turn right onto North Hoosac Avenue (this will turn into Massachusetts Avenue after crossing into North Adams).

3.8 Bear left at the Y-intersection to stay on Massachusetts Avenue (a road to the right passes under a railroad bridge).
You will soon come into North Adams, a city of sprawling brick mill buildings and row houses mixed with a contemporary-arts center and historical museum.

5.2 At the traffic light, continue straight.

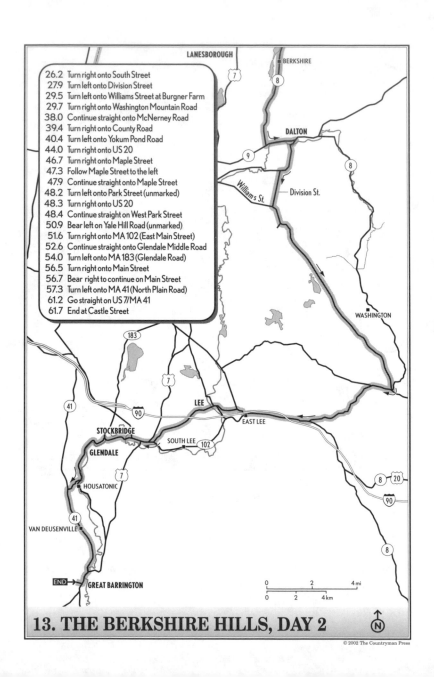

26.2	Turn right onto South Street
27.9	Turn left onto Division Street
29.5	Turn left onto Williams Street at Burgner Farm
29.7	Turn right onto Washington Mountain Road
38.0	Continue straight onto McNerney Road
39.4	Turn right onto County Road
40.4	Turn left onto Yokum Pond Road
44.0	Turn right onto US 20
46.7	Turn right onto Maple Street
47.3	Follow Maple Street to the left
47.9	Continue straight onto Maple Street
48.2	Turn left onto Park Street (unmarked)
48.3	Turn right onto US 20
48.4	Continue straight on West Park Street
50.9	Bear left on Yale Hill Road (unmarked)
51.6	Turn right onto MA 102 (East Main Street)
52.6	Continue straight onto Glendale Middle Road
54.0	Turn left onto MA 183 (Glendale Road)
56.5	Turn right onto Main Street
56.7	Bear right to continue on Main Street
57.3	Turn left onto MA 41 (North Plain Road)
61.2	Go straight on US 7/MA 41
61.7	End at Castle Street

13. THE BERKSHIRE HILLS, DAY 2

5.5 At the next traffic light, turn right onto Eagle Street.

5.7 At this traffic light, head straight onto MA 8A.
Use caution in this busy downtown area.

8.2 Bear left on Church Street, which turns into East Road as you cross into Adams.
The house where Susan B. Anthony was born is marked with a small plaque. It is in a neighborhood of modest homes on the rural outskirts of Adams.

12.4 Continue straight onto Bucklin Road.

13.6 Turn right onto MA 116.

13.9 Turn left onto Wells Road.

17.8 At the traffic light in Cheshire, turn left onto MA 8.
Cheshire is a quiet community of dairy farms along the Cheshire Reservoir. The cheese monument in the village commemorates when local farmers sent a massive 1,235-pound block of cheddar to Washington, D.C. as a gift to President Thomas Jefferson in 1801.

25.0 At the traffic light, turn left onto MA 9.
Use caution when crossing through this very busy intersection.

26.2 At the traffic light in Dalton, turn right onto South Street.
Crane & Company's 1846 old stone mill features exhibits tracing the history of American papermaking from the late 1700s. Five generations of the Crane family have run this company, the exclusive supplier of paper to the U.S. Mint.

27.9 At the traffic light, turn left onto Division Street.

29.5 Turn left onto Williams Street at Burgner Farm.

29.7 Turn right onto Washington Mountain Road.
The reward for the strenuous 1.5-mile climb is a secluded, flat ridgetop road through October Mountain State Forest. At 16,127 acres, it's the largest state forest in Massachusetts. You'll descend into Becket, home to the prestigious Jacob's Pillow Dance Festival, the nation's oldest dance festival.

38.0 Continue straight onto McNerney Road.

39.4 Just before the stop sign at MA 8 (Main Street), turn right onto County Road.

40.4 Turn left onto Yokum Pond Road.

44.0 At the stop sign, turn right onto US 20.

46.7 Turn right onto Maple Street, following the sign for October Mountain State Forest.

47.3 Follow Maple Street to the left.

47.9 At the stop sign, continue straight onto Maple Street.

48.2 Turn left onto Park Street (unmarked).

48.3 At the stop sign, turn right onto US 20.

48.4 At the stop sign, continue straight on West Park Street (US 20 turns right), passing by downtown Lee.
The road climbs into the rural hills above Lee and Stockbridge.

50.9 Just past the Stockbridge town line, bear left on Yale Hill Road (unmarked).

51.6 At the stop sign, turn right onto MA 102 (East Main Street).
Pass through the historic village of Stockbridge.

52.6 On the outskirts of the village, continue straight onto Glendale Middle Road (MA 102 continues to the right).

54.0 At the stop sign, turn left onto MA 183 (Glendale Road).

56.5 In the village of Housatonic, turn right onto Main Street.

56.7 Bear right to continue on Main Street (Pleasant Street is on the left).

57.3 At the stop sign, turn left onto MA 41 (North Plain Road).

61.2 At the traffic light, go straight on US 7/MA 41.

61.7 The ride ends at Castle Street in downtown Great Barrington.

Bicycle Shops

Foster Harland Inc., 15 Bridge Street, Great Barrington; 413-528-0564
Ordinary Cycles, 247 North Street, Pittsfield; 413-442-7225
The Spoke, 279 Main Street (MA 2), Williamstown; 413-458-3456

The Sports Corner, 61 Main Street, North Adams; 413-664-8654
Berkshire Outfitters, MA 8, Adams; 413-743-5900

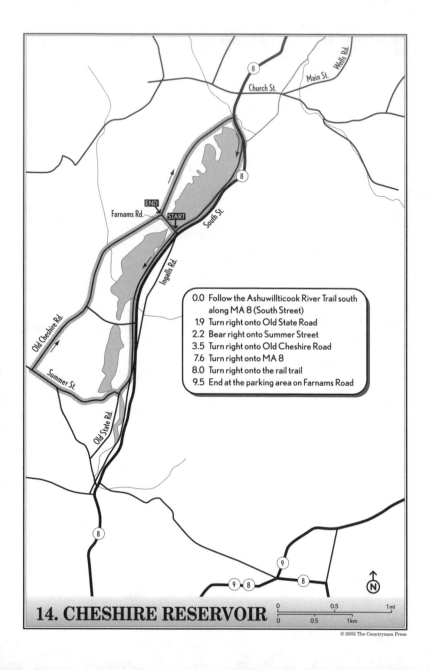

0.0 Follow the Ashuwillticook River Trail south
     along MA 8 (South Street)
1.9 Turn right onto Old State Road
2.2 Bear right onto Summer Street
3.5 Turn right onto Old Cheshire Road
7.6 Turn right onto MA 8
8.0 Turn right onto the rail trail
9.5 End at the parking area on Farnams Road

14. CHESHIRE RESERVOIR

0   0.5   1 mi
0   0.5   1 km

© 2002 The Countryman Press

Cheshire Reservoir

- **DISTANCE:** 9.5 miles
- **TERRAIN:** Flat with some short rolling sections
- **DIFFICULTY:** Easy
- **RECOMMENDED BICYCLE:** Touring/road bike

This pleasant loop is the shortest—and one of the easiest—tours in the book. It follows the 4-mile-long shoreline of Cheshire Reservoir at the foot of the rugged peaks in the Mount Greylock State Reservation.

Part of the ride follows the Ashuwillticook River Trail, a paved bike path that runs 10 miles from Lanesborough to Adams along MA 8 and the Hoosic River. Plans are underway to extend the path in both directions. The bike path is popular with walkers, in-line skaters, and cyclists. Use caution when riding and let people know of your presence when approaching them from behind.

The ride begins in Cheshire on the eastern side of Mount Greylock. MA 8 is a main north-south route through the Berkshires but generally less busy than US 7 on the other side of the mountain. Nevertheless, the bike path is a welcome alternative to riding along with traffic. The village has the usual collection of historic buildings, but its notoriety lies in something quiet different: cheese.

In 1801 President Jefferson was presented with the Great Cheshire Cheese, a 1,235-pound, barrel-shaped wedge of cheddar

The Ashuwillticook River Trail is a popular bicycle route along the Cheshire Reservoir.

that farmers made from one day's entire milk production. It was shipped to Albany by oxen, then by boat, to Washington, D.C.

Jefferson gave some cheese to everyone in the White House and sent $200 to the Cheshire farmers. In keeping with tradition, Cheshire residents made a smaller scale, 21-pound wheel of cheese and sent it to President Clinton in 1993.

At the southern tip of the reservoir is Berkshire, a tiny roadside community named for the hills and county it resides in.

DIRECTIONS FOR THE RIDE
The ride begins at the parking area on Farnams Road, adjacent to the reservoir and the rail trail.

0.0 Take the Ashuwillticook River Trail, following it south along MA 8 (South

Street).

1.9 At the second street crossing, turn right onto Old State Road.

2.2 Just past the tip of the reservoir, bear right onto Summer Street.
This quiet back road climbs past sprawling upland farms high above the reservoir.

3.5 Turn right onto Old Cheshire Road.
The road follows a high ridge for about 1 mile before descending through woods.

7.6 At the stop sign, turn right onto MA 8.

8.0 Turn right onto the rail trail.

9.5 The ride ends at the parking area on Farnams Road.

Bicycle Shops

Berkshire Outfitters, MA 8, Adams; 413-743-5900
Ordinary Cycles, 247 North Street, Pittsfield; 413-442-7225

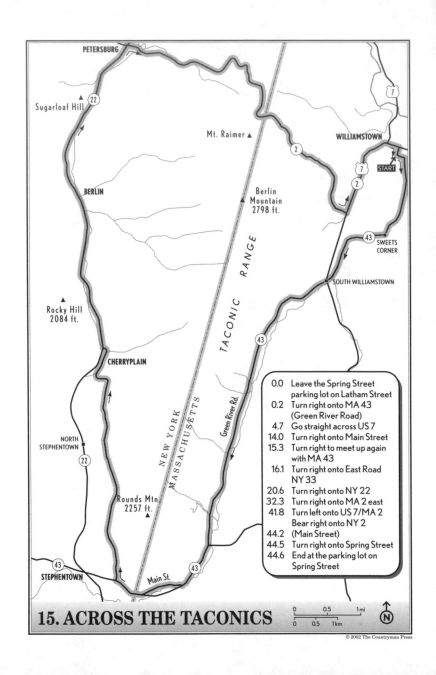

PETERSBURG

Sugarloaf Hill ▲ 22

Mt. Raimer ▲

WILLIAMSTOWN

7

2

7

START

2

BERLIN

Berlin
Mountain
2798 ft. ▲

43 SWEETS
CORNER

SOUTH WILLIAMSTOWN

Rocky Hill
2084 ft. ▲

TACONIC RANGE

43

CHERRYPLAIN

NEW YORK

MASSACHUSETTS

Green River Rd.

NORTH
STEPHENTOWN
22

Rounds Mtn.
2257 ft. ▲

0.0	Leave the Spring Street parking lot on Latham Street
0.2	Turn right onto MA 43 (Green River Road)
4.7	Go straight across US 7
14.0	Turn right onto Main Street
15.3	Turn right to meet up again with MA 43
16.1	Turn right onto East Road NY 33
20.6	Turn right onto NY 22
32.3	Turn right onto MA 2 east
41.8	Turn left onto US 7/MA 2 Bear right onto NY 2
44.2	(Main Street)
44.5	Turn right onto Spring Street
44.6	End at the parking lot on Spring Street

43

STEPHENTOWN

Main St.

43

15. ACROSS THE TACONICS

0   0.5   1 mi
0   0.5   1 km

N

© 2002 The Countryman Press

Across the Taconics: Williamstown to New York

- **DISTANCE**: 44.6 miles
- **TERRAIN**: Rolling hills with a challenging climb through the Taconic Range
- **DIFFICULTY**: Strenuous
- **RECOMMENDED BICYCLE**: Touring/road bike

Berkshire County's rural northwest corner is home to one of the nation's most prestigious small liberal arts colleges. Williams College was founded in 1793 with funds bequeathed by Colonel Ephraim Williams Jr., one of the village's original settlers who was killed at the Battle of Lake George. Colonel Williams earmarked the money with one condition: the settlement change its name from West Hoosuck to Williamstown.

The campus is dotted with handsome brick buildings, classic examples of Federal architecture. The surrounding countryside contributes equally to the beauty of the campus, from the bucolic farmland along the Green River to the rolling hills that rise to the nearby summit of Mount Greylock, the state's tallest peak.

Henry David Thoreau—a man with deep connections to the mountain—visited the college in the 19th century and spoke of Mount Greylock and the wisdom he believed people gained by exploring mountains:

It were as well
to be educated in the shadow

of a mountain as in more classic shade.
Some will remember, no doubt,
not only that they went to college,
but that they went to the mountain.

The Sterling and Francine Clark Art Institute boasts an outstanding collection of 19th-century American and European works, dominated by French impressionism (including more than 30 Renoirs). The museum is built upon the personal acquisitions of Singer sewing machine heir Robert Sterling Clark and his wife, Francine, from the early 20th century. The Williams College Museum of Art has a respected collegiate art collection, with permanent holdings dominated by American 19th- and 20th-century paintings and a wealth of paintings by Maurice Prendergast.

Spring Street is the town's main shopping avenue, crammed

A historic farm in the foothills of the Taconic Range

with shops, cafés, and galleries, and bustling with students and visitors.

You will leave Williamstown on MA 43, a high rolling road through a landscape of farm fields dotted with barns and silos that will take you into New York. After following the Little Hoosic River through an upland farming valley to Petersburg, you'll begin the arduous 5-mile climb into the Taconics. The imposing ridges extend from the northwestern corner of the state, along the western border with New York, and then south to Connecticut. The state line crosses the summit near Petersburg Pass; from there it's a rewarding 4-mile descent into Williamstown.

DIRECTIONS FOR THE RIDE
The ride begins at the public parking lot at the end of Spring Street in the center of Williamstown.

0.0 Leave the Spring Street parking lot on Latham Street.

0.2 At the stop sign, turn right onto MA 43 (Green River Road).

4.7 At the stop sign and blinking traffic light in South Williamstown, go straight across US 7.
The Store at Five Corners is an 18th-century general store selling specialty foods and deli items.

7.6 Cross into the town of Hancock.
The road cuts a swath through rolling hills and a valley of farms and pastures.

14.0 Turn right onto Main Street, passing through the tiny village of Hancock.
The village street is lined with old homes, a church, and a bed & breakfast.
OPTION: Stay on MA 43 if you wish not to make the detour.

15.3 Turn right to meet up again with MA 43.

15.5 Cross into New York State and the town of Stephentown.

16.1 Turn right onto East Road/NY 33.
This scenic road winds through the woods and up and down hills dotted with silos, barns, and meadows.

20.6 At the stop sign, turn right onto NY 22.

This is a busy main road but has a wide shoulder to ride on. The rolling road follows the Little Hoosic River and passes through wide farmland.

24.0 Pass through the center of Berlin.
There is a convenience store in town.

32.3 In Petersburg, turn right onto US 2 east, just after passing under a stone bridge.
You'll ride through a small village before heading into the mountains on the Taconic Trail. The road begins rolling but gradually turns into a strenuous climb. The route affords views into the valley below where you began in Petersburg. Use caution on the narrow shoulder.

37.8 At the summit is Taconic Ridge State Forest.
This scenic overlook is a good rest stop before beginning the 4-mile descent into Williamstown. The work is done here, so you can enjoy the views on the way down. The Williamstown town line is just below the summit on the other side.

41.8 At the stop sign, turn left onto US 7/MA 2.

44.2 Bear right onto MA 2 (Min Street) at the Williams College campus.

44.5 Turn right onto Spring Street.

44.6 Turn into the parking lot at the bottom of Spring Street to end the ride.

Bicycle Shops

Mountain Goat Bicycle Shop, 130 Water Street, Williamstown; 413-458-8445

The Spoke, 279 Main Street (MA 2), Williamstown; 413-458-3456

THE
HAMPSHIRE
HILLS

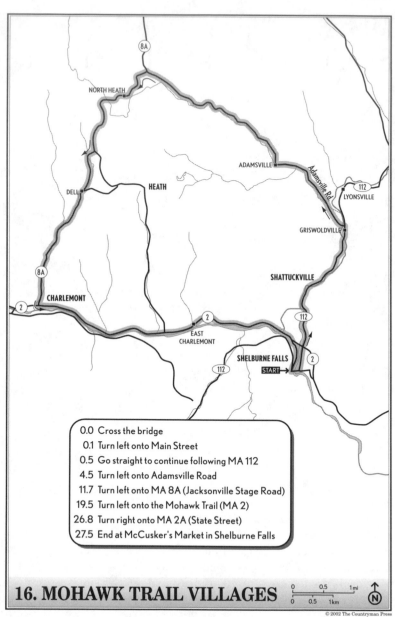

0.0 Cross the bridge

0.1 Turn left onto Main Street

0.5 Go straight to continue following MA 112

4.5 Turn left onto Adamsville Road

11.7 Turn left onto MA 8A (Jacksonville Stage Road)

19.5 Turn left onto the Mohawk Trail (MA 2)

26.8 Turn right onto MA 2A (State Street)

27.5 End at McCusker's Market in Shelburne Falls

16. MOHAWK TRAIL VILLAGES

0   0.5   1mi

0   0.5   1km

Mohawk Trail Villages:
Shelburne Falls and Charlemont

- **DISTANCE:** 27.5 miles
- **TERRAIN:** Rolling hills with a couple moderate climbs
- **DIFFICULTY:** Moderate
- **RECOMMENDED BICYCLE:** Touring/road bike

This tour connects the villages of Charlemont and Shelburne Falls with the high backcountry between the Mohawk Trail and the Vermont border. The ride follows the North River into a remote area of woodland, orchards, farms, and meadows. You'll return to Shelburne Falls on the Mohawk Trail, a popular tourist road evolved from a Native American footpath once used for travel and trade between Boston and Dutch settlements in New York. It was widened by early European settlers and now is a two-lane highway, particularly busy during the peak foliage season in October.

The ride begins at McCusker's Market, a popular meeting place in the lively village of Shelburne Falls. The former Odd Fellows Hall sits at the heart of this arts community created by two towns, Buckland and Shelburne, and linked by a bridge over the Deerfield River.

The river is the scene of the village's most popular sites. Just south of the bridge is a series of ancient potholes, swirling rock formations worn by the gradual flooding and receding of the Deerfield River during and after the glacial periods. Moving stones and whirlpools eroded the granite and created smooth holes ranging in diameter from 5 inches to 39 feet.

When a trolley bridge over the river closed in the early 1900s, the Shelburne Falls Women's Club created a footpath lined with flowers. Each spring the Bridge of Flowers erupts into a profusion of flowers and foliage that cascades over the sides of the arched bridge and draws thousands of visitors.

DIRECTIONS FOR THE RIDE

The ride begins at McCusker's Market on the Buckland side of the Deerfield River at the Bridge of Flowers. Parking can be found along the street or at the municipal parking lot on Main Street across the river.

0.0 From McCusker's Market, cross the bridge to the Shelburne side of the river.

0.1 Turn left onto Main Street at the sign for MA 112 and Colrain.

McCusker's Market is a lively deli and natural food store in Shelburne Falls.

0.5 Go straight to continue following MA 112 as it heads north along the Deerfield River.
The road joins the North River as the Deerfield River branches west along the Mohawk Trail.

4.5 Turn left onto Adamsville Road, crossing the North River on a green metal bridge.
This country road on the west branch of the North River (the east branch follows MA 112 into Vermont) is lined with cornfields and farms. It winds gently through quiet countryside for about 4 miles before making a long steady climb into steeper hills.

11.7 Turn left onto MA 8A (Jacksonville Stage Road).
Follow this twisting rural highway south to Charlemont.

19.3 Pass the Bissell Covered Bridge next to the road.
This historic covered bridge spans the Mill River.

19.5 At the stop sign in Charlemont, turn left onto the Mohawk Trail (MA 2).
You can pick up supplies at Wells Corner Country Store. The Mohawk Trail rolls gently along the Deerfield River on the way to Shelburne Falls. Many of the roadside homesteads were built when the valley was first farmed in the 18th century.

26.8 Turn right onto MA 2A (State Street) to return to Shelburne Falls.

27.5 The ride ends at McCusker's Market.

Bicycle Shops

Bicycle World, 104 Federal Street (MA 5/MA 10), Greenfield; 413-774-3701
Bicycles Unlimited, 322 High Street, Greenfield; 413-772-2700

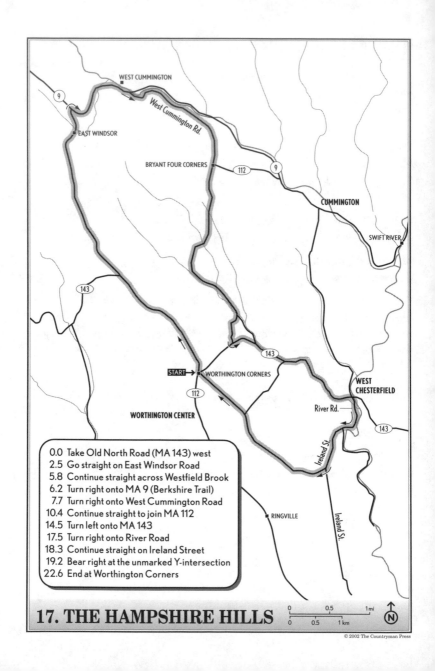

WEST CUMMINGTON

9

EAST WINDSOR

West Cummington Rd.

BRYANT FOUR CORNERS   112   9

CUMMINGTON

SWIFT RIVER

143

143

START → ■ WORTHINGTON CORNERS

112

WORTHINGTON CENTER

WEST CHESTERFIELD

River Rd.   143

Ireland St.

RINGVILLE

Ireland St.

0.0 Take Old North Road (MA 143) west
2.5 Go straight on East Windsor Road
5.8 Continue straight across Westfield Brook
6.2 Turn right onto MA 9 (Berkshire Trail)
7.7 Turn right onto West Cummington Road
10.4 Continue straight to join MA 112
14.5 Turn left onto MA 143
17.5 Turn right onto River Road
18.3 Continue straight on Ireland Street
19.2 Bear right at the unmarked Y-intersection
22.6 End at Worthington Corners

17. THE HAMPSHIRE HILLS

0   0.5   1mi
0   0.5   1 km

N

© 2002 The Countryman Press

The Hampshire Hills

- **DISTANCE:** 22.6 miles
- **TERRAIN:** Rolling hills with a few steep climbs
- **DIFFICULTY:** Strenuous
- **RECOMMENDED BICYCLE:** Touring/road bike

This is a hilly but beautiful ride through the forested backcountry of Hampshire County, one of the state's most desolate and least-visited areas. You'll climb and descend rural roads to hilltop farms and villages overlooking the Westfield River Valley.

The ride begins in Worthington Corners, a quiet crossroads village deep in the Hampshire Hills. The Corners Grocery is an old-fashioned general store built in 1860 on a tiny green. A church, historic inn, and several antique homes complete the village.

Hidden in the lofty hills between Cummington and Worthington Corners is the William Cullen Bryant Homestead, a grand 23-room mansion on a 246-acre hilltop spread. It was built in 1783 by Bryant's family and became the writer's summer estate in the mid-1800s. His descendents lived at the homestead until 1965.

Bryant is known as the American Wordsworth for his writings, particularly on nature. His poem *Thanatopsis* was dubbed the "best poem produced in America." Relics from Bryant's career as a poet and editor of the *New York Evening Post* fill the meticulously restored house, which is maintained by the Trustees of Reservations and open to visitors on summer weekends.

From these heights you'll descend toward Chesterfield, turning before the village to follow the west branch of the Westfield River. Down a side trail is Chesterfield Gorge, a narrow canyon enclosed by sheer granite walls. A hiking trail offers dramatic views of the rock walls and the river far below. The gorge is part of an extensive natural recreation area surrounding the Westfield River, a designated national wild and scenic river whose waters rage in springtime and flow peacefully in the dry summer months. Atlantic salmon, duck, bear, bobcat, otter, beaver, and wild turkey live in the area.

The dirt section of River Road adjacent to this route is popular with mountain bikers. From the gorge, it leads south into Gilbert Bliss State Forest and the Knightville Dam area. Cycling is allowed only on the road.

DIRECTIONS FOR THE RIDE

The ride begins at Corners Grocery in the village of Worthington Corners, at the junction of MA 143 and MA 112.

0.0 Take Old North Road (MA 143) west out of Worthington Corners. *The highlights of this quaint village are the clapboard general store and the elegant Worthington Inn, a 1780 homestead on a 60-acre hilltop surrounded by open fields.*

2.5 Go straight on East Windsor Road (MA 143 continues to the left). *East Windsor Road becomes Cole Street as you cross into Cummington, then Worthington Road in Windsor. This is a long descent through the woods, gradual at times, more rapid at others.*

5.8 In East Windsor, continue straight across Westfield Brook, following the sign for MA 9.

6.2 At the stop sign, turn right onto MA 9 (Berkshire Trail). *Enjoy the stunning hill views as you make another long descent.*

7.7 Turn right onto West Cummington Road. *The road is flat at first, winding along the Westfield River, before climbing steeply into the hills. Ancient trees and old homesteads line these very lightly traveled upland roads that seem untouched by time.*

A rural road along the Westfield River

10.4 At the stop sign at the top of the hill (Bryant Four Corners), continue straight to join MA 112.

The William Cullen Bryant Homestead is on the far side of a meadow at this rural junction, down a short side road. Enjoy the long descent from here with panoramic views of the surrounding hills.

14.5 Turn left onto MA 143, following the signs toward Chesterfield.
The road twists and descends for another 3 miles.

17.5 Just before the river, turn right onto River Road, following the sign to Chesterfield Gorge.
This narrow back road follows the Westfield River.

18.3 At the turnoff for Chesterfield Gorge, continue straight on Ireland Street.
Ireland Street turns into Old Post Road as you cross into Worthington. One of the steepest climbs on the route takes you to farmland and forest high above the river.

19.2 At the unmarked Y-intersection, bear right and continue climbing for another 0.5 mile before beginning the descent into Worthington Corners.

22.6 The ride ends in the center of Worthington Corners.

Bicycle Shops

Ordinary Cycles, 247 North Street, Pittsfield; 413-442-7225

Plaine's Bike Ski Snowboard, 55 West Housatonic Street, Pittsfield; 413-499-0294

Northampton Bicycle, 319 Pleasant Street, Northampton; 413-586-3810

18

New Boston to Otis

- **DISTANCE**: 22.3 miles
- **TERRAIN**: Flat stretches and low hills; several miles of rolling dirt roads
- **DIFFICULTY**: Moderate
- **RECOMMENDED BICYCLE**: Mountain bike, hybrid, or road bike with knobby tires

The ride connects the villages of New Boston (part of the town of Sandisfield) and Otis along a network of quiet, often dirt roads. Even the two state roads that form the backbone of this route—MA 57 and MA 8—are relatively lightly traveled.

These towns started as farming communities before industry came to western Massachusetts in the mid-1800s. Gristmills, tanneries, and iron forges once thrived here along the banks of the Farmington River, while shops produced furniture, carriages, rakes, and other goods.

The New Boston Inn, on the corner of MA 8 and MA 57 in Sandisfield, is listed as a national historic site. The 1737 stagecoach stop is considered Berkshire County's oldest inn. Today it's a busy inn, restaurant, and tavern.

Otis was named in 1810 for Harrison Grey Otis, former Boston mayor and speaker of the Massachusetts House of Representatives. The route passes just south of the village center, which is a short detour on MA 8.

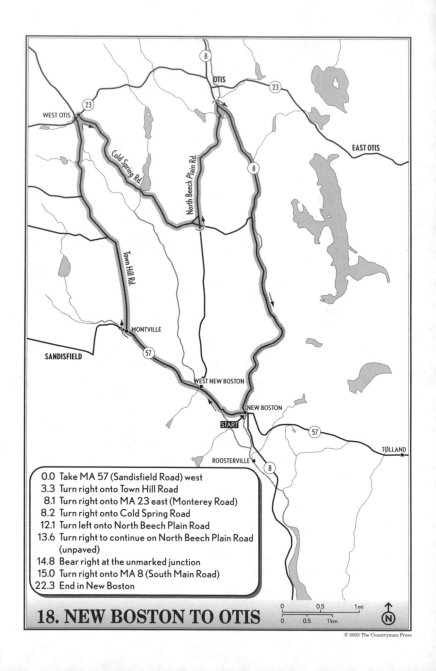

0.0 Take MA 57 (Sandisfield Road) west
3.3 Turn right onto Town Hill Road
8.1 Turn right onto MA 23 east (Monterey Road)
8.2 Turn right onto Cold Spring Road
12.1 Turn left onto North Beech Plain Road
13.6 Turn right to continue on North Beech Plain Road (unpaved)
14.8 Bear right at the unmarked junction
15.0 Turn right onto MA 8 (South Main Road)
22.3 End in New Boston

18. NEW BOSTON TO OTIS

© 2002 The Countryman Press

A quiet dirt rood in Tolland State Forest in Otis

Much of the ride follows dirt roads through the nearly 10,000 acres of woodland protected by Tolland State Forest. In January 1776, General Henry Knox led a group of troops and artillery from Fort Ticonderoga to Boston to help fight the British. In his journal, Knox described the rugged area, which was then part of Tyringham: "Reached (Tyringham) after having climbed mountains (from) which we might almost have seen all the kingdoms of the Earth."

A mountain bike, hybrid, or road bike with knobby tires is best for this ride; the dirt roads are hard-packed but hilly.

DIRECTIONS FOR THE RIDE

Begin the ride in New Boston; there is a small dirt parking area on MA 8 just north of the New Boston Inn. The New Boston Store in the village center has food and drinks; there is a similar store and café in Otis.

0.0 From the parking area, head toward the inn and take MA 57 (Sandisfield Road) west out of New Boston.
The road follows the Buck River for the most part, so it is relatively flat with undulating dips and rises.

3.3 Turn right onto Town Hill Road.
Immediately begin a short, steep climb that will become more gradual as it heads into Sandisfield State Forest.

6.0 The road surface turns to hard-packed dirt for about 1.5 miles; use caution on the descents.

8.1 At the stop sign, turn right onto MA 23 east (Monterey Road).

8.2 Take an immediate right onto Cold Spring Road.
This isolated stretch is mostly wooded, with some farmland and a few open meadow views around Upper Spectacle Pond. The stone walls along the way hint at the profusion of farmland here centuries ago.

12.1 Turn left onto North Beech Plain Road (dirt).

13.6 Just past an old cemetery, turn right to continue on North Beech Plain Road.
About 0.5 mile down this dirt road is a sign marking the site where Revolutionary War troops led by General Henry Knox marched across the road.

14.8 Bear right at the unmarked junction of a paved road.

15.0 At the stop sign, turn right onto MA 8 (South Main Road).
This mostly flat stretch follows the winding curves of the Farmington River. A convenience store and café in Otis is a short distance north on MA 8.

22.3 The ride ends in New Boston.

Bicycle Shops

Berkshire Bike & Blade, 326 Stockbridge Road (US 7), Great Barrington; 413-528-5555

Foster Harland Inc., 15 Bridge Street, Great Barrington; 413-528-0564

Custom Cycle, 88 Elm Street, Westfield; 413-568-6036

19

Beartown State Forest via Tyringham

- **DISTANCE:** 30.6 miles
- **TERRAIN:** Rolling to steep hills; flat sections along the Housatonic River; a 1-mile dirt road
- **DIFFICULTY:** Moderate
- **RECOMMENDED BICYCLE:** Touring/road bike

Tyringham is a remote village in a farming valley surrounded by mountains. Despite its beauty, few tourists reach this area, perhaps because of its inaccessibility. Besides the main north-south route through town, the roads east and west are mostly dirt.

From South Lee, the route follows the Housatonic River through farm fields before climbing into the heavily wooded hills above the valley floor. A Shaker community on Jerusalem Road was active from 1792 until the late 1800s.

You'll enjoy a picture-postcard view descending into Tyringham. In the center of town, a neat white Greek Revival church sits on a rise with an ancient burial ground behind it. Also on the descent is Tyringham Cobble, 206 acres of steep wooded slopes maintained by the Trustees of Reservations. The rocky summit of the 400-foot hill provides dramatic views into valley. The cobble was once farmed on its upper slopes, but forest has since reclaimed it. A trail leads through woods that open to a hillside meadow, a popular stop for migrating birds and monarch butterflies.

Mark Twain was among the artists and writers who summered

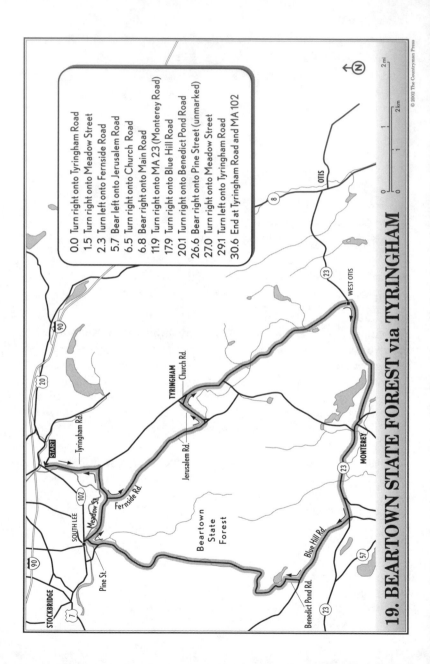

0.0 Turn right onto Tyringham Road
1.5 Turn right onto Meadow Street
2.3 Turn left onto Fernside Road
5.7 Bear left onto Jerusalem Road
6.5 Turn right onto Church Road
6.8 Bear right onto Main Road
11.9 Turn right onto MA 23 (Monterey Road)
17.9 Turn right onto Blue Hill Road
20.1 Turn right onto Benedict Pond Road
26.6 Bear right onto Pine Street (unmarked)
27.0 Turn right onto Meadow Street
29.1 Turn left onto Tyringham Road
30.6 End at Tyringham Road and MA 102

© 2002 The Countryman Press

19. BEARTOWN STATE FOREST via TYRINGHAM

here; he donated a complete set of his books to the public library. Santarella Museum and Gardens, north of the village on Main Road, is a studio and sculpture garden exhibiting the work of local artists. Sculptor Sir Henry Hudson Kitson's 19th-century studio is also known as the Gingerbread House because of its whimsical architecture and thatchlike shingled roof.

The quiet road through Beartown State Forest is winding and rolling in parts, long and flat in others, and crisscrossed with trails. The Appalachian Trail passes through the 10,879-acre forest, crossing the 2,112-foot summit of Mount Wilcox. This vast tract rises from Monterey, stretches north on a high flat road, and then drops to the Housatonic River in South Lee.

Monterey is a quiet village on the fringe of Beartown State Forest that was once a community of dairy farms. It was part of Tyringham until 1847. The clapboard Monterey General Store at the center of the village makes a good rest stop.

DIRECTIONS FOR THE RIDE

The ride begins in South Lee, at the junction of MA 102 and Tyringham Road, just south of the Massachusetts Turnpike (US 90). Start from the small dirt parking area across the street from the Lee Travel Plaza.

0.0 From the parking area, turn right onto Tyringham Road.
This flat quiet road follows the Housatonic River, first through a small neighborhood, then past broad farm fields with nice views of the Berkshire Hills.

1.5 Turn right onto Meadow Street.
This pretty road cuts through more fields stretching north and south as you ride toward the hills.

2.3 Turn left onto Fernside Road.
The road climbs gradually into the woods and turns to dirt after 1 mile as you enter Tyringham; the town line is designated by a plain stone marker. This beautiful road feels miles away from civilization; you'll see only a few antique barns and homesteads, and miles of twisting stone walls cut through rocky fields.

5.7 Bear left onto Jerusalem Road.
On the corner here you will see Hav's Farm with its barns full of jersey cows. Just past the farm the road heads sharply downhill. On the descent you will begin to see

West Brook rushes through Beartown State Forest on its way to the Housatonic River.

the village of Tyringham below. You will also pass the trailhead for Tyringham Cobble.

6.5 Turn right onto Church Road.
On the corner is the white clapboard 1782 Tyringham School House, used today as a municipal building. You'll then pass the 1844 Greek Revival United Church of Christ and its graveyard, which were visible from the road above the village.

6.8 At the yield sign, bear right onto Main Road.

11.9 At the stop sign, turn right onto MA 23 (Monterey Road).

15.5 Pass through the tiny village of Monterey.
The white-steepled Monterey Meetinghouse, a rambling clapboard general store and a small white grange building, which houses the town hall, line the road. For supplies, there is also a small store a couple miles ahead on MA 23.

17.9 Turn right onto Blue Hill Road, just past the green sign for Beartown State Forest.
The road climbs past old homesteads with views of the hills.

20.1 Near the top of the hill, turn right onto Benedict Pond Road.

20.5 Continue on the forest road past Benedict Pond.
The road through the forest is pocketed with rough pavement. Make the descents slowly, especially on a road bike. The road follows West Brook, which feeds into the Housatonic River. Along the way you'll pass the remnants of a Civilian Conservation Corps (CCC) camp, clustered in a clearing with a stand of massive evergreens and a stone fireplace. The CCC workers used the camp from 1933 to 1942.

26.6 After leaving the state forest, bear right at the Y-intersection onto Pine Street (unmarked).

27.0 Turn right onto Meadow Street.
This is a flat stretch through open farmland on the banks of the Housatonic River.

29.1 At the stop sign, turn left onto Tyringham Road.

30.6 The ride ends at the parking area on Tyringham Road and MA 102.

Bicycle Shops

The Arcadian Shop, 91 Pittsfield Road (US 7), Lenox; 1-800-239-3391

Main Street Sports & Leisure, 18 Main Street (MA 7A), Lenox; 413-637-4407

Mean Wheels Bike Shop, 57A Housatonic Street, Lenox; 413-637-0644

River Roads: Shelburne Falls to Vermont

- **DISTANCE:** 54.8 miles
- **TERRAIN:** Low to moderate hills; rolling terrain along the Deerfield and North Rivers
- **DIFFICULTY:** Moderate to strenuous
- **RECOMMENDED BICYCLE:** Touring/road bike

The ride leaves the town of Shelburne Falls on the Mohawk Trail (MA 2) and explores the quiet river roads heading north into Vermont. The Mohawk Indians used this route as a passage from the Hudson River to the Connecticut River Valley during the French and Indian War. Souvenir shops and Indian trading posts line the road, reminiscent of the era of automobile touring. It has been an official scenic road since 1914; remarkably, the tiny villages just off the route are preserved and quiet.

Past Charlemont you will notice the hills that rise precipitously above the Deerfield River. This is the eastern edge of the rugged Hoosac Range, the Berkshire Barrier that frustrated settlers and thwarted efforts at commerce between Boston and Albany. The solution came with the Hoosac Tunnel, a massive project that blasted a 4.7-mile-long passage below the mountain range. It cost nearly two hundred lives and $15 million, an exorbitant sum in the 19th century. It was the first engineering project to use explosive nitroglycerine to blast through a mountain. The eastern portal of the tunnel is near the railroad tracks past the Zoar Picnic Area on

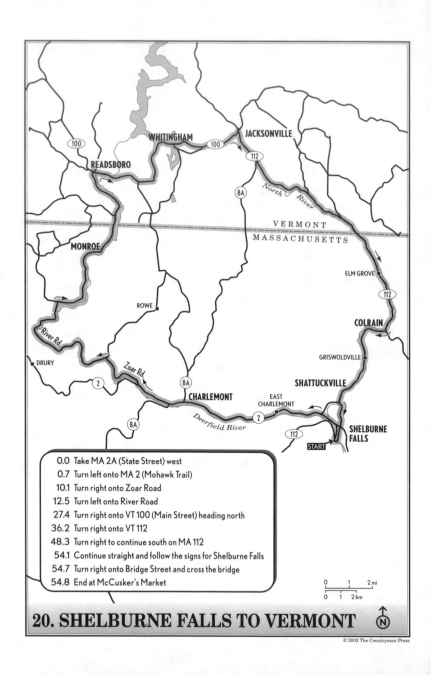

0.0 Take MA 2A (State Street) west

0.7 Turn left onto MA 2 (Mohawk Trail)

10.1 Turn right onto Zoar Road

12.5 Turn left onto River Road

27.4 Turn right onto VT 100 (Main Street) heading north

36.2 Turn right onto VT 112

48.3 Turn right to continue south on MA 112

54.1 Continue straight and follow the signs for Shelburne Falls

54.7 Turn right onto Bridge Street and cross the bridge

54.8 End at McCusker's Market

20. SHELBURNE FALLS TO VERMONT

River Road. You'll also pass the tiny village of Monroe Bridge, with the massive decommissioned Yankee Rowe Nuclear Power Plant looming over the river.

In Vermont, you'll pass through Readsboro, Whitingham, and Jacksonville on the scenic highway that made *Car & Driver*'s list of "Ten Best Roads in America." VT 100 is the state's longest highway; in its 200 miles from the Massachusetts border through the Green Mountains there are only three stoplights. Readsboro was busy in the 1880s with paper and pulp mills on the Deerfield River; today it's a quiet roadside village. Whitingham is the birthplace of Mormon prophet Brigham Young. Two sites in town commemorate the native son who founded Salt Lake City. The Jacksonville General Store sits at the center of a classic Vermont village, which consists of old homes, a bed & breakfast, and a church.

Back in Massachusetts, Colrain sits along MA 112 and the east branch of the North River. In the 1800s this was a bustling community, with residents working on sheep farms and in cotton mills and the town's iron foundry. Today it's a quiet roadside village surrounded by more than one thousand acres of state forest. The Colrain Fair in mid-September draws many visitors. Another gem is Green Emporium, an eclectic bistro occupying a 150-year-old former Methodist church.

Residents of this remote community have a proud history of activism. In 1812 they protested the British navy's seizure of American ships—despite Colrain's distance from the sea—by a flag raising that is still done today. Villagers built three forts as protection from French and Indian forces. The first schoolhouse in the country to fly the American flag is still here.

DIRECTIONS FOR THE RIDE

The ride begins at McCusker's Market in Shelburne Falls. There is a public parking lot on the other side of the river on Main Street. There are food stores in Shelburne Falls and Charlemont, and general stores in Whitingham and Jacksonville, Vermont.

0.0 From McCusker's Market, take MA 2A west (State Street) out of the village, following the Deerfield River.

0.7 At the stop sign, turn left onto MA 2 (Mohawk Trail).
This busy road has a wide shoulder. You'll pass trading posts, centuries-old farm-houses of clapboard and brick, river outfitters, and antiques shops.

8.0 Pass through the village of Charlemont.
Historic homes and a church line the road; A. L. Avery & Son General Store and Well's Corner Country Store have food and supplies.

10.1 Turn right onto Zoar Road, following the sign to Rowe and Monroe.

12.5 Cross a small bridge, then turn left onto River Road.
The road narrows considerably as it follows railroad tracks and the Deerfield River through one of the most remote areas of the state.

13.4 Pass the Zoar Picnic Area.
You'll climb a couple hills that bring you high above the river.

The Bridge of Flowers in Shelburne Falls is a profusion of color from spring to fall.

23.1 Pass by the village of Monroe Bridge.

24.4 The unmarked state line of Vermont is along the shore of the Sherman Reservoir.

26.8 Enter Readsboro, Vermont.

27.4 At the stop sign, turn right onto VT 100 (Main Street), heading north.
This winding climb takes you through the southern portion of Green Mountain National Forest, into rolling upland meadows and woods with long views of the southern Green Mountains.

32.6 Pass through the village of Whitingham.
You can pick up supplies at the general store. A couple miles out of the village, begin the descent to Jacksonville.

36.2 In Jacksonville, turn right onto VT 112.
This beautiful and remote stretch of country road follows the curves of the North River as it flows south into Massachusetts.

48.3 In Colrain, turn right to continue south on MA 112.
There is a small grocery store on the outskirts of the village.

54.1 Where MA 112 goes left, continue straight and follow the signs for Shelburne Falls.

54.7 At the stop sign, turn right onto Bridge Street and cross the bridge to the Buckland side of the river.

54.8 The ride ends at McCusker's Market in Shelburne Falls.

Bicycle Shops

Bicycle World, 104 Federal Street (MA 5/MA 10), Greenfield; 413-774-3701
Bicycles Unlimited, 322 High Street, Greenfield; 413-772-2700

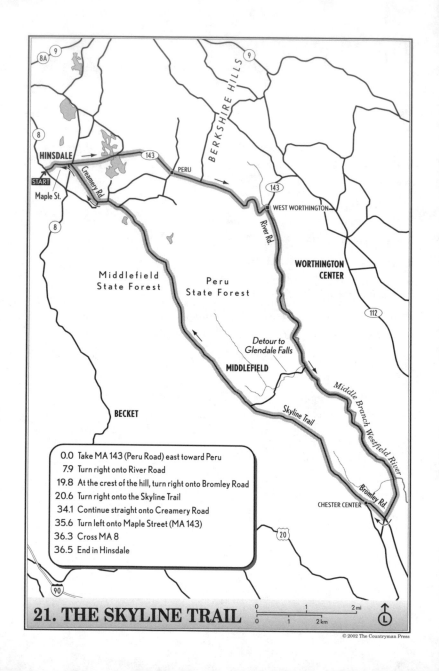

0.0 Take MA 143 (Peru Road) east toward Peru
7.9 Turn right onto River Road
19.8 At the crest of the hill, turn right onto Bromley Road
20.6 Turn right onto the Skyline Trail
34.1 Continue straight onto Creamery Road
35.6 Turn left onto Maple Street (MA 143)
36.3 Cross MA 8
36.5 End in Hinsdale

21. THE SKYLINE TRAIL

© 2002 The Countryman Press

The Skyline Trail

- **DISTANCE:** 36.5 miles
- **TERRAIN:** Rolling hills and a couple sustained climbs
- **DIFFICULTY:** Strenuous
- **RECOMMENDED BICYCLE:** Touring/road bike

To some visitors, these lofty villages are more reminiscent of Vermont's isolated Northeast Kingdom than southern New England. Part of the route follows the scenic Skyline Trail, which traces the edge of the high Berkshire Plateau and offers dramatic panoramas of the hills to the west.

The ride begins in the manufacturing town of Hinsdale on the east branch of the Housatonic River. A cluster of historic Federal and Greek Revival town buildings center in downtown. The 1868 Gothic-style public library is the work of architect Leopold Eidlitz, who designed the state capitol in Albany.

The village of Peru was settled in 1767 and aptly named for the mountainous South American country. At 2,295 feet it's the highest town in Massachusetts. Settlers liked the upland spot for the safety it provided from Indians occupying the river valleys. The tidy white church—the highest in New England—and the library and historical museum are among the handful of simple buildings in this tiny hilltop community.

A respite from hills comes by following the middle branch of the Westfield River through a remote valley before climbing once again

There are several working farms along the Skyline Trail.

to Chester and Middlefield, farming villages on the Skyline Trail. A general store in the center of Middlefield is a good rest stop.

DIRECTIONS FOR THE RIDE
The ride begins in downtown Hinsdale, south of Dalton on MA 8.

0.0 From the Hinsdale Public Library on MA 8, take MA 143 (Peru Road) east toward Peru.
The 4-mile climb to Peru begins immediately. Among the old homes lining the street are the Stritch Outdoor Sculpture Garden and the Maplewood Bed and Breakfast.

4.2 At the hilltop, pass through Peru.
The Peru Library & Museum, a church, and a tiny triangle of green make up the village. Begin a long descent from here as you continue on MA 143.

7.9 Turn right onto River Road.
There are a few miles of rough pavement along this little-used road; use caution.

13.4 Pass the detour to Glendale Falls on unmarked Clark Wright Road.
Glendale Brook cascades 175 feet over a rocky precipice before joining the middle branch of the Westfield River. The 60-acre nature preserve includes a trail to the base of the falls, remnants of the 18th-century Glendale Farm, and the stone foundation of an old gristmill. It's an arduous climb to the falls, but a worthwhile rest stop.

18.5 Begin the steep climb out of the river valley.

19.8 At the crest of the hill, turn right onto Bromley Road.

20.6 In Chester Center, turn right onto the Skyline Trail.
Chester Center is a quiet village with a church and several historic homes, which gives way to sloping meadows, farms, orchards, and long views along the Skyline Trail.

27.0 Pass through Middlefield.
The olive clapboard Middlefield General Store is a good rest stop at the center of this little village.

34.1 Continue straight onto Creamery Road.

35.6 At the stop sign, turn left onto Maple Street (MA 143).

36.3 At the traffic light, cross MA 8.

36.5 The ride ends in the center of Hinsdale.

Bicycle Shops

Ordinary Cycles, 247 North Street, Pittsfield; 413-442-7225

Plaine's Bike Ski Snowboard, 55 West Housatonic Street, Pittsfield; 413-499-0294

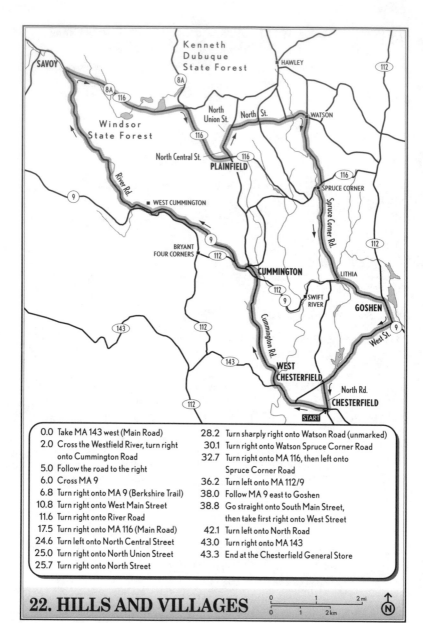

0.0	Take MA 143 west (Main Road)
2.0	Cross the Westfield River, turn right onto Cummington Road
5.0	Follow the road to the right
6.0	Cross MA 9
6.8	Turn right onto MA 9 (Berkshire Trail)
10.8	Turn right onto West Main Street
11.6	Turn right onto River Road
17.5	Turn right onto MA 116 (Main Road)
24.6	Turn left onto North Central Street
25.0	Turn right onto North Union Street
25.7	Turn right onto North Street

28.2	Turn sharply right onto Watson Road (unmarked)
30.1	Turn right onto Watson Spruce Corner Road
32.7	Turn right onto MA 116, then left onto Spruce Corner Road
36.2	Turn left onto MA 112/9
38.0	Follow MA 9 east to Goshen
38.8	Go straight onto South Main Street, then take first right onto West Street
42.1	Turn left onto North Road
43.0	Turn right onto MA 143
43.3	End at the Chesterfield General Store

22. HILLS AND VILLAGES

0   1   2 mi
0   1   2 km

N

© 2002 The Countryman Press

Hills and Villages

- **DISTANCE:** 43.3 miles
- **TERRAIN:** Rolling and steep hills; a flat stretch along the Westfield River
- **DIFFICULTY:** Strenuous
- **RECOMMENDED BICYCLE:** Touring/road bike

This tour of four rural New England villages follows hills linked by gentle valley terrain. Steep climbs take you to high open countryside with rewarding views of the hills that seem to radiate in all directions.

You'll begin in the hilltop town of Chesterfield. Among the historic buildings are the 1848 town hall, a small historical museum, the 1835 Congregational Church, and a restored 19th-century gristmill. The village of Cummington is equally lofty, best known for the restored homestead of poet and 19th-century resident William Cullen Bryant. The writer best known for nature poems such as *Thanatopsis* and *To a Waterfowl,* and as editor of the *New York Observer,* turned his boyhood home into an elegant gentleman's farm in the late 1800s. It's maintained by the Trustees of Reservations and open to the public.

A respite from the hills comes as you follow the Westfield River on its winding course through the wooded hills of Windsor State Forest and Notchview Reservation, named for the notch the river cuts into the hills. It's a peaceful stretch of gentle terrain with many good places to stop and rest along the riverbank. The lofty villages of Plainfield and Goshen are surrounded by spectacular upland farmland.

This area is dotted with sugarhouses; when riding from late February through April look for the telltale aluminum buckets hanging in clusters around the trunks of maple trees along the road. During sugaring season visitors can see demonstrations and sample maple products. Some of these farms still use horses and oxen to gather the sap.

DIRECTIONS FOR THE RIDE

The ride begins in Chesterfield at the Chesterfield General Store just west of the village on MA 143. There are also stores selling food and supplies in Cummington and Goshen.

0.0 Leave Chesterfield on MA 143 west (Main Road).
The ride begins with a steep 2-mile descent.

The Hampshire Hills are dotted with upland farms.

2.0 Cross the Westfield River, then turn right onto Cummington Road.
This very rural back road winds through the woods; use caution on the occasional rough areas of pavement.

5.0 Just past the Cummington Fairgrounds, follow the road to the right.
Just past the fairgrounds is a sugarhouse that's open to the public during sugaring season in early spring. The Cummington Fair has been held here every August for more than 135 years.

6.0 At the stop sign, cross MA 9 to head toward Cummington.
This side road is lined with antique homes, a white clapboard church, and a small historical museum. The Kingman Tavern is a restored tavern, post office, and general store that is open to visitors on summer weekends.

6.8 At the stop sign, turn right onto MA 9 (Berkshire Trail).
This main but quiet road follows the Westfield River past the Old Creamery Grocery and the fieldstone Bryant Free Library, named for local poet William Cullen Bryant.

10.8 Turn right onto West Main Street, following the signs for West Cummington and Windsor State Forest.

11.6 Turn right onto River Road at the edge of the village.
This scenic and lightly traveled road twists along the Westfield River and passes through more than 3,000 acres of pristine forest.

17.5 Turn right onto MA 116 (Main Road).

24.6 In Plainfield, turn left onto North Central Street.
Fewer than five hundred people live in this historic farming community of white clapboard homes, a village school, and a stately 19th-century Congregational Church topped by a dome instead of the classic New England spire.

25.0 Just past the cemetery, turn right onto North Union Street.

25.7 Turn right onto North Street.

28.2 Just past the farm at the top of a long climb, make a sharp right onto Watson Road (unmarked).
Farms, fields, and old maples line either side of the road; use caution on the twisty descent.

30.1 Turn right onto Watson Spruce Corner Road.
The South Face Farm sugarhouse is on this corner.

32.7 Turn right onto MA 116, then immediately left onto Spruce Corner Road.

36.2 At the stop sign, turn left onto MA 112/9.
Begin the 1.5-mile climb to Goshen.

38.0 Follow MA 9 east to Goshen at the junction where MA 112 continues left.
There is a general store in this hilltop village where you can pick up supplies.

38.8 Just past the Goshen Historical Society, go straight onto South Main Street, then take the first right onto West Street.
This rural road through the hill country between Goshen and Chesterfield turns into Damon Pond Road as you cross the town line.

42.1 At the stop sign, turn left onto North Road.

43.0 At the stop sign in Chesterfield, turn right onto MA 143.

43.3 The ride ends at the Chesterfield General Store.

Bicycle Shops

Ordinary Cycles, 247 North Street, Pittsfield; 413-442-7225

Berkshire Outfitters, MA 8, Adams; 413-743-5900

Northampton Bicycle, 319 Pleasant Street, Northampton; 413-586-3810

23

Ashfield to Shelburne Falls

- **DISTANCE:** 22.8 miles
- **TERRAIN:** Rolling hills; a 1-mile dirt road
- **DIFFICULTY:** Moderate
- **RECOMMENDED BICYCLE:** Touring/road bike

This ride features the historic villages of Ashfield and Shelburne Falls, linked by back roads through rolling farm country. Ashfield is a charming New England enclave of vintage Colonial clapboard homes, white-spired churches, and a general store. Perhaps it owes part of its charm to the fact that it receives few visitors compared to the popular Berkshire towns to the west. (Two of these visitors were the parents of Cecil B. DeMille: The future Hollywood director was born in a hotel on Main Street.) Like a well-kept secret, this area is tucked away in the remote hills between the Berkshires and the Connecticut River, crossed by rural roads through forested hills and rocky upland pastures.

Most of Ashfield's Main Street is a national historic district, including the 1827 St. John's Episcopal Church, complete with Gothic arch windows, and the 1856 Greek Revival Congregational Church. The steeple of the 1812 town hall—once a church—resides over the village and marks where the ride begins. This close-knit community of 1,700 is home to many craftspeople, artists, and writers; it even publishes its own newspaper. If you're here in late September or October you might catch the town's lively fall festival.

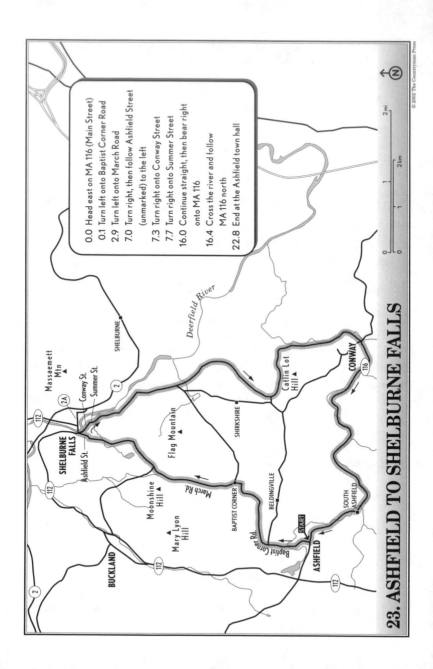

0.0 Head east on MA 116 (Main Street)
0.1 Turn left onto Baptist Corner Road
2.9 Turn left onto March Road
7.0 Turn right, then follow Ashfield Street (unmarked) to the left
7.3 Turn right onto Conway Street
7.7 Turn right onto Summer Street
16.0 Continue straight, then bear right onto MA 116
16.4 Cross the river and follow MA 116 north
22.8 End at the Ashfield town hall

© 2002 The Countryman Press

23. ASHFIELD TO SHELBURNE FALLS

The narrow streets of Shelburne Falls bustle with galleries, shops, artists' studios, and cafés. Most visitors come to see the ancient glacial potholes near Salmon Falls, and the Bridge of Flowers, an old trolley bridge that was transformed into a 400-foot-long footpath when trolley service ended in the 1920s. A profusion of tumbling flowerbeds bloom continuously from spring to fall; in summer the flowers reach their peak and cascade dramatically above the river.

The glacial potholes on the north side of the river are a natural phenomenon. A wide expanse of rock has been smoothed by water and time, leaving swirls of gray, white, black, and brown. The rock is gneiss, volcanic ash, and sand similar to granite. Fifty potholes were created during the glacial age, ranging in size from tiny saucer-size holes to 39 feet in diameter.

Beautiful country roads head south from Shelburne Falls through hills dotted with farms, orchards, and thick forest. From Conway, you'll follow the South River on MA 116, a road that hugs the bank of this twisting river and climbs steadily to Ashfield.

DIRECTIONS FOR THE RIDE

The ride starts at the town hall in Ashfield on MA 116. Park along the street. McCusker's Market in Shelburne Falls is a health food store with a good deli.

0.0 From the town hall, head east on MA 116 (Main Street).

0.1 Turn left onto Baptist Corner Road.
This flat, winding lane passes through a quiet neighborhood of farmhouses, an old cemetery, and a bed & breakfast before entering the forested hills northeast of the village.

2.9 Turn left onto March Road.
After climbing a short steep hill, the road narrows and turns into a well-maintained dirt lane for about 1 mile. The road turns into Bray Road at the Buckland town line and descends toward Shelburne Falls.

7.0 At the stop sign, turn right, then follow Ashfield Street (unmarked) as it bends sharply left.
The metal bridge spanning the Deerfield River in Shelburne Falls comes into view.

The ancient glacial potholes in the Deerfield River in Shelburne Falls

7.3 In front of McCusker's Market, make a sharp right turn onto Conway Street.
The road here follows the river upstream, past the Lamson & Goodnow Manufacturing Company, a 19th-century brick complex that was one of the nation's largest producers of cutlery during the Civil War. It still manufactures cutlery and tools that are sold in an outlet store at the site.

7.7 Turn right onto Summer Street (you'll be facing a dead-end road).
Past the ball fields the road climbs away from the river and through rural hills on the way to Conway.

16.0 At the stop sign, continue straight, then bear right onto MA 116.
Old homes line the road for a short time before giving way to woods on the outskirts of Conway. To see the village center, take a short detour left on MA 116.

16.4 Cross the river and follow MA 116 north as it bends to the right.
The road back to Ashfield follows the South River.

22.8 The ride ends in front of the town hall in the center of Ashfield.

Bicycle Shops

Bicycle World, 104 Federal Street (MS 5/MA 10), Greenfield; 413-774-3701
Bicycles Unlimited, 322 High Street, Greenfield; 413-772-2700

THE
PIONEER
VALLEY

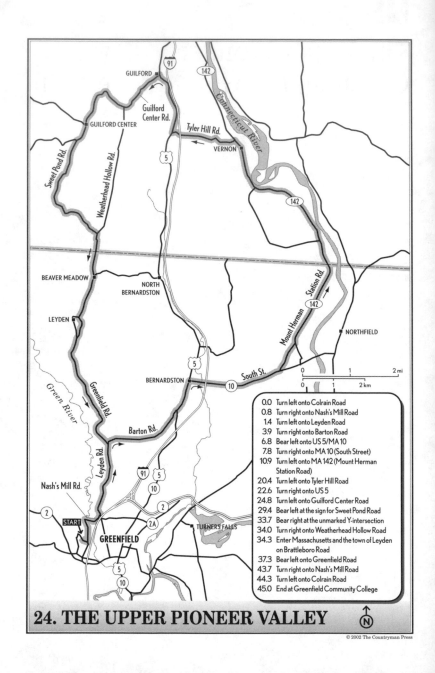

GUILFORD

91

142

Connecticut River

Guilford
Center Rd.

GUILFORD CENTER

Tyler Hill Rd.

VERNON

Sweet Pond Rd.

Weatherhead Hollow Rd.

5

142

BEAVER MEADOW

NORTH
BERNARDSTON

LEYDEN

Mount Herman Station Rd.

142

NORTHFIELD

Green River

Greenfield Rd.

5

BERNARDSTON

South St.

10

Barton Rd.

0   1   2 mi

0   1   2 km

Leyden Rd.

91

5

10

Nash's Mill Rd.

2

2

START

2A

TURNERS FALLS

GREENFIELD

5

10

Distance	Instruction
0.0	Turn left onto Colrain Road
0.8	Turn right onto Nash's Mill Road
1.4	Turn left onto Leyden Road
3.9	Turn right onto Barton Road
6.8	Bear left onto US 5/MA 10
7.8	Turn right onto MA 10 (South Street)
10.9	Turn left onto MA 142 (Mount Herman Station Road)
20.4	Turn left onto Tyler Hill Road
22.6	Turn right onto US 5
24.8	Turn left onto Guilford Center Road
29.4	Bear left at the sign for Sweet Pond Road
33.7	Bear right at the unmarked Y-intersection
34.0	Turn right onto Weatherhead Hollow Road
34.3	Enter Massachusetts and the town of Leyden on Brattleboro Road
37.3	Bear left onto Greenfield Road
43.7	Turn right onto Nash's Mill Road
44.3	Turn left onto Colrain Road
45.0	End at Greenfield Community College

24. THE UPPER PIONEER VALLEY

N

The Upper Pioneer Valley: Greenfield to Guilford, Vermont

- **DISTANCE:** 45.0 miles
- **TERRAIN:** Flat sections mixed with rolling and steep climbs; 5 miles of dirt roads
- **DIFFICULTY:** Strenuous
- **RECOMMENDED BICYCLE:** Hybrid

This ride starts in Greenfield, the seat of Franklin County and commercial center of the upper Pioneer Valley, and heads north into Vermont. This northernmost section of the wide valley along the Connecticut River below Vermont remains a rural area of quiet farmland despite the busy commercial strip of US 5/MA 10 and I-91 cutting a swath through it. Most of the ride is on back roads, some very remote dirt ones along the border of the two states. These are relatively flat and gently rolling scenic rural roads lined with horse, dairy, and Christmas tree farms.

The Pioneer Valley is named for its history of early settlement. Since the rugged Berkshires hindered travel to the west, farmers began working the fertile lowland along the Connecticut River. It remains a rural landscape of wide fields dotted with farms and small towns. The northern part of the valley near Vermont is only a few miles wide; beyond that the floodplains rise into gentle hills that gradually drift into the Berkshires.

In the late 1600s, farmers planted these fertile fields on the outskirts of Greenfield, known as Greenfield Meadows. Some of the earliest houses still exist as private homes, including the Moses Arms, built in 1776 by a Revolutionary War captain.

Industry boomed along the Connecticut River in the 19th century. Greenfield's prime location at the confluence of the Connecticut and Green Rivers helped the mill town thrive. The J. Russell Company was the nation's first cutlery factory; its best-known product was the Green River buffalo-skinning knife. The green in downtown Greenfield is framed by historic commercial buildings, as well as restaurants, stores, and two bike shops.

The Colonial village of Guilford, Vermont, is surrounded by hilly backcountry, laced with a network of remote dirt roads. Thick woods open to the occasional upland farm or rocky pasture as the roads drift back toward Massachusetts.

DIRECTIONS FOR THE RIDE

The ride begins at Greenfield Community College, at the junction of Colrain Street and Colrain Road in Greenfield. There are food stores in Bernardston, and in Vernon and Guilford, Vermont.

0.0 At the entrance to the community college, turn left onto Colrain Road.
The ride begins on a flat country road flanked by farm fields, produce stands, and a small grocery store.

0.8 Turn right onto Nash's Mill Road.
On this road, look for a historical marker commemorating Captain Turner, the leader of area settlers who was killed by Indians after the battle at the Great Falls of the Connecticut.

1.4 At the stop sign, turn left onto Leyden Road.

3.9 Turn right onto Barton Road.
The road winds up a gradual climb into a quiet neighborhood.

6.4 Enter the town of Bernardston.

6.8 At the stop sign, bear left onto US 5/MA 10.
Use caution through this busy section.

7.8 Turn right onto MA 10 (South Street).
Head north through the center of town, past Streeters General Store just before

A network of remote dirt roads connects the Pioneer Valley of southern Vermont.

crossing over I-91. This is a heavily traveled main road with a wide shoulder to ride on.

10.9 Turn left onto MA 142 (Mount Herman Station Road).
Head north toward Vernon and Brattleboro, Vermont. Immediately enter the town of Gill, then pass through Northfield on this winding country road. Enjoy the sweeping views of the hills and ridges to the north dotted with farmland.

14.8 Cross into the town of Vernon at the Vermont state line.
The hills seem to become even more dramatic as you head north into Vermont. The ridgeline to the east is New Hampshire, on the other side of the Connecticut River. There is a gas station/convenience store along the way; make sure water bottles are filled since it's the last place to stop for several miles.

20.4 Turn left onto Tyler Hill Road.
This is a steep winding climb into the woods.

22.2 Cross over I-91.
Just past the highway, use caution as the road winds steeply downhill.

22.6 At the stop sign, turn right onto US 5.
Descend north toward the village of Guilford.

24.8 Turn left onto Guilford Center Road.
The red clapboard Guilford Country Store is a good rest stop before heading back to Massachusetts.

29.4 Bear left at the sign for Sweet Pond Road.
The pavement ends as this quiet road winds up rolling hills—steep in places—then descends through the woods past Sweet Pond State Park.

33.7 Bear right at the unmarked Y-intersection.
Pass to the right of a small house at this intersection, then descend past a cemetery on the left.

34.0 At the stop sign, turn right onto Weatherhead Hollow Road.

34.3 Cross into Massachusetts and the town of Leyden on Brattleboro Road.
This rolling country road turns into Greenfield Road at the state line, where it is paved.

36.8 A detour on the right leads to the tiny village of Leyden.

37.3 At the stop sign, bear left onto Greenfield Road.
The road winds through rural countryside, descending toward Greenfield.

43.7 Turn right onto Nash's Mill Road.

44.3 At the stop sign, turn left onto Colrain Road.

45.0 Turn right into the parking lot of Greenfield Community College to end the ride.

Bicycle Shops

Bicycle World, 104 Federal Street (US 5/ MA 10), Greenfield; 413-774-3701
Bicycles Unlimited, 322 High Street, Greenfield; 413-772-2700

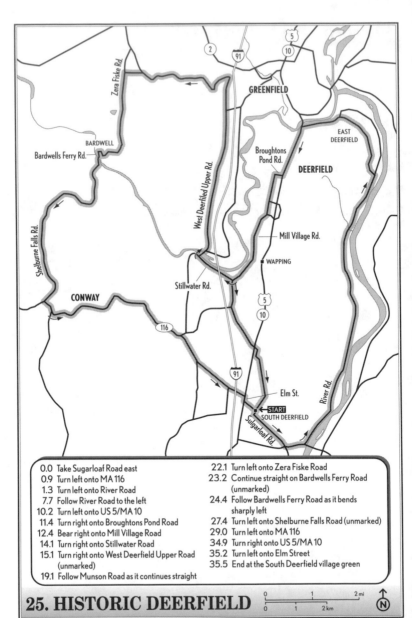

Zera Fiske Rd.

GREENFIELD

EAST
DEERFIELD

BARDWELL

Bardwells Ferry Rd.

Broughtons
Pond Rd.

DEERFIELD

West Deerfield Upper Rd.

Mill Village Rd.

Shelburne Falls Rd.

WAPPING

Stillwater Rd.

CONWAY

116

91

Elm St.

River Rd.

START
SOUTH DEERFIELD

Sugarloaf Rd.

0.0 Take Sugarloaf Road east
0.9 Turn left onto MA 116
1.3 Turn left onto River Road
7.7 Follow River Road to the left
10.2 Turn left onto US 5/MA 10
11.4 Turn right onto Broughtons Pond Road
12.4 Bear right onto Mill Village Road
14.1 Turn right onto Stillwater Road
15.1 Turn right onto West Deerfield Upper Road (unmarked)
19.1 Follow Munson Road as it continues straight

22.1 Turn left onto Zera Fiske Road
23.2 Continue straight on Bardwells Ferry Road (unmarked)
24.4 Follow Bardwells Ferry Road as it bends sharply left
27.4 Turn left onto Shelburne Falls Road (unmarked)
29.0 Turn left onto MA 116
34.9 Turn right onto US 5/MA 10
35.2 Turn left onto Elm Street
35.5 End at the South Deerfield village green

25. HISTORIC DEERFIELD

0   1   2 mi
0   1   2 km

N

Historic Deerfield

- **DISTANCE:** 35.5 miles (about 20 miles, omitting the hills section)
- **TERRAIN:** Flat stretches with rolling to challenging hills
- **DIFFICULTY:** Strenuous (easy if omitting the hills section)
- **RECOMMENDED BICYCLE:** Touring/road bike

Historic Deerfield is a living museum in the Connecticut River Valley, a collection of vintage 18th- and 19th-century homes surrounded by thousands of acres of farmland. It's many people's vision of quintessential New England and arguably one of the best-preserved Colonial villages in America.

Deerfield was settled in 1669 by English farmers, first as an outpost village, then as a prosperous agricultural center in the 18th century. Georgian and Federal-style homes—many predating 1850—are among Deerfield's beautiful antique gems stretching along the 1-mile village road, known as The Street, a grand avenue lined with 200-year-old elms. Visitors can tour 14 buildings full of Colonial-era artifacts, and historical exhibits contain tens of thousands of historic household objects and decorative arts used and produced since 1650.

Deerfield's picture postcard image belies its unsettled history. There were more than 30 attacks on the town, beginning just a few years after the village was settled. The Bloody Brook Massacre, a battle during King Philip's War between Indians and settlers in

1675, took 64 lives and burned the original settlement. In February 1704, Indians led by French troops raided and burned the village in a dawn attack that left 50 townspeople dead. More than 100 others were taken hostage and marched to Canada; 20 didn't survive the 300-mile journey. The door of the former Sheldon-Hawks House is preserved in the Memorial Hall Museum; the tomahawk marks in the door are a reminder of the quiet village's turbulent history.

The surrounding landscape is perfect for riding—the broad floodplain of the Deerfield River ensures some easy flat roads—surrounded by thousands of acres of farmland, meadows, and forest. The Deerfield River joins the Connecticut River east of the village. The Pocumtuck Indians relied on these rivers for trade, travel, and a vital food source; settlers used the river for waterpower and to water their livestock and crops. The fertile valley attracted farmers due to what was lacking: the profusion of fieldstone that prevailed in New England and was the bane of farmers trying to carve out an existence in the often harsh and unforgiving landscape.

Native American legend suggests that the great spirit Manitou turned a giant beaver into stone, thus creating the 7-mile Pocumtuck Ridge that sits about 700 feet above the river valley. You'll climb through a hardwood forest of maple, beech, and birch trees, full of mountain laurel that reaches its peak in June. Back roads crisscross rugged hills and pass upland farms around the remote and wildly beautiful Bardwells Ferry Road.

Most visitors to this area—more than a million a year—don't miss a stop to the Yankee Candle Company in South Deerfield on US 5/MA 10. The sprawling complex includes a car museum, a toy factory, a Bavarian village, and, of course, the ubiquitous scented candles.

DIRECTIONS FOR THE RIDE

Start in the center of South Deerfield, just east of US 5/MA 10. The ride begins near the village green at the junction of Main and Sugarloaf Streets, where there is parking on the street.

There is an option for an easy ride (about 20 miles) that passes through

Old Deerfield without climbing through the hills. At the end of The Street in Old Deerfield, bear right onto Mill Village Road and follow it to US 5/MA 10. Cross the intersection and take Main Street into South Deerfield.

0.0 Take Sugarloaf Road east out of South Deerfield toward the Mount Sugarloaf State Reservation.

0.9 At the traffic light, turn left onto MA 116.
Mount Sugarloaf State Reservation is a 532-acre park with an observation tower at the mountaintop, affording sweeping views of the Connecticut River, the Berkshire Hills, and the Pioneer Valley. The 652-foot monadnock gets its name from the sandstone rock called Sugarloaf Arkose. King Philip reportedly surveyed Deerfield from here before the Bloody Brook Massacre in the mid-1600s.

1.3 Just before the bridge crossing the Connecticut River, turn left onto River Road.

Old Deerfield has some of the nation's best-preserved Colonial homes.

The road is flat with gentle rolling sections and passes through farm fields that flank the riverbank.

7.7 At the sharp bend, follow River Road to the left.

10.2 At the stop sign, turn left onto US 5/MA 10.

11.4 Turn right onto Broughtons Pond Road, following the signs to Historic Deerfield.
Historic Deerfield was founded in 1952 by Henry and Helen Flynt, whose son attended Deerfield Academy. The couple purchased the homes and financed their restoration and preservation. Some of the standouts include the Asa Stebbins House, an elegant Federal-style brick home built in 1799; the Hinsdale and Anna Williams House, first built in the mid-1700s, renovated in Georgian style in 1818, then with Federal-style additions; and the 1743 Sheldon-Hawks House, with an intricate Connecticut Valley–style doorway.

12.4 At the fork, bear right onto Mill Village Road.
This very rural area has flat farm fields on either side of the road as you follow the river.

14.1 Just past the dairy farm, turn right onto Stillwater Road. (For the optional short loop, continue on Mill Village Road, cross US 5/MA 10, and follow Main Street into South Deerfield to end the ride.)
Continue following the Deerfield River and pass under I-91.

15.1 Turn right onto West Deerfield Upper Road (unmarked).
There is a steep climb here that rolls at the top through a rural area with scattered homes.

18.4 Cross the Greenfield town line. The road changes to Munson Road.

19.1 Follow Munson Road as it continues straight (the main road will bear to the right).
A challenging 2-mile climb begins here; the road will change to South Shelburne Road as you cross back into Deerfield and climb through the woods.

22.1 Turn left onto Zera Fiske Road.
Look for the turn after making a descent. This rolling road passes through isolated farmland with long views.

23.2 Continue straight on Bardwells Ferry Road (unmarked).
Use caution on the descents on this wildly isolated road.

24.4 Cross the railroad tracks and follow Bardwells Ferry Road as it bends sharply left above the South River.
You will cross the river on a narrow iron bridge, a popular spot for anglers, then wind back up through South River State Forest. At the top is more open hilltop with long scenic rural views of farmland ringed with hills.

27.4 At the stop sign, turn left onto Shelburne Falls Road (unmarked).

29.0 At the stop sign, turn left onto MA 116.
You'll pass through the tiny village of Conway as you head east to return to South Deerfield. The ornate Marshall Field Memorial Library was donated by Conway resident-turned-department-store-tycoon Marshall Field.

34.9 At the traffic light, turn right onto US 5/MA 10.

35.2 At the first traffic light, turn left onto Elm Street.
Yankee Candles have been produced at the South Deerfield headquarters since 1969. The sprawling complex is the world's largest candle factory and store.

35.5 The ride ends at the village green in South Deerfield.

Bicycle Shops

Bicycle World, 104 Federal Street (US 5/MA 10), Greenfield; 413-774-3701

Bicycles Unlimited, 322 High Street, Greenfield; 413-772-2700

Northampton Bicycle, 319 Pleasant Street, Northampton; 413-586-3810

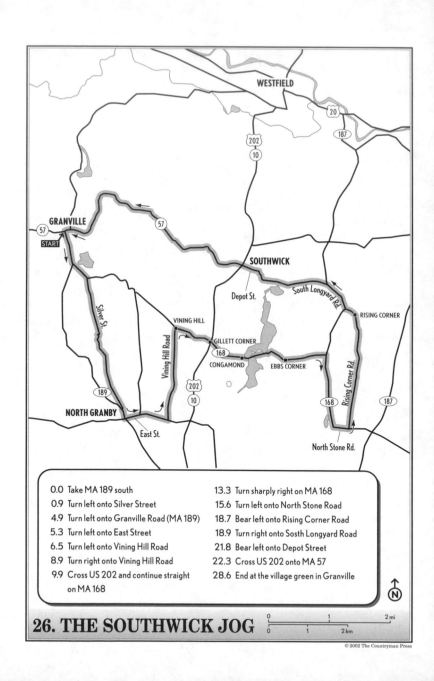

WESTFIELD

20

187

202
10

GRANVILLE

57

57

START

SOUTHWICK

Depot St.

South Longyard Rd.

RISING CORNER

Silver St.

VINING HILL

Vining Hill Road

GILLETT CORNER

168

CONGAMOND

EBBS CORNER

Rising Corner Rd.

187

189

202
10

168

NORTH GRANBY

East St.

North Stone Rd.

0.0 Take MA 189 south	13.3 Turn sharply right on MA 168
0.9 Turn left onto Silver Street	15.6 Turn left onto North Stone Road
4.9 Turn left onto Granville Road (MA 189)	18.7 Bear left onto Rising Corner Road
5.3 Turn left onto East Street	18.9 Turn right onto Sosth Longyard Road
6.5 Turn left onto Vining Hill Road	21.8 Bear left onto Depot Street
8.9 Turn right onto Vining Hill Road	22.3 Cross US 202 onto MA 57
9.9 Cross US 202 and continue straight on MA 168	28.6 End at the village green in Granville

N

26. THE SOUTHWICK JOG

0   1   2 mi

0   1   2 km

© 2002 The Countryman Press

The Southwick Jog

- **DISTANCE:** 28.6 miles
- **TERRAIN:** Rolling hills with flat sections along the Congamond Lakes
- **DIFFICULTY:** Moderate
- **RECOMMENDED BICYCLE:** Touring/road bike

There is a distinguishing mark on western Massachusetts's otherwise perfectly horizontal southern boundary with Connecticut— a small protrusion about 2.5 square miles in size just to the west of the Connecticut River. Anyone who looks at a map of the state surely sees it, but few can explain it. The abnormality, known as the Southwick Jog, sprang from a 17th-century land surveying mishap.

In 1642 the Massachusetts Bay Colony hired a pair of surveyors—Solomon Saffery and Nathaniel Woodward—to survey the colony's southern border with Connecticut. After working west from Boston, they encountered an Indian war party east of the Connecticut River. The pair decided to backtrack and paddle up the Connecticut River to avoid a potentially dangerous confrontation. When they resumed the survey, they mistakenly began several miles too far south, creating a dispute over this area that lasted more than 160 years.

A settlement over the pocket of land was reached in 1793 that gave Southwick control of the Congamond Lakes, which the town needed to power its mills. The river towns of Suffield and Enfield were incorporated into Connecticut.

In the past two decades, many housing developments have sprung up amid acres of farm fields, changing Southwick from a quiet agricultural village to a bedroom community of residents who commute to nearby Springfield and Hartford. A few working farms producing tobacco and other crops still blanket this flat fertile plain, however. Look for the long tobacco barns and white gauzelike tents that shade the tobacco plants from the hot sun.

The ride begins in Granville Village, a quiet community tucked into the Berkshire foothills and surrounded by farmland and thousands of acres of state forest. The Granville Country Store has been the village cornerstone since John Murray Gibbons first opened the doors in 1851. A cheese aficionado who was particular about properly aged cheddar, Gibbons made his own in the store cellar. When the demand for Gibbons Cheddar—later known as Granville Cellar Aged Cheddar—became overwhelming, he found a small dairy in New York State to provide his milk supply. Customers short on cash paid for their purchases with goods, trading everything from produce and grain to livestock for some of the local artisan cheese.

The store left the hands of the Gibbons family in 1935, but cheddar is still made exclusively for the store using the making and aging processes in Gibbons' recipe.

DIRECTIONS FOR THE RIDE

Begin the ride in Granville Village (not to be confused with Granville Center or West Granville, both on MA 57 to the west); there is a small dirt parking area next to the Granville Country Store on the village green. Parking is also available at the post office, at the eastern end of the historic district on MA 57.

0.0 Leave Granville Village on MA 189 south, heading toward Connecticut.

0.9 Turn left onto Silver Street.
This road is a mix of woods and housing developments on either side of the state line; a testament to the population surge in an area that 20 years ago was largely agricultural.

4.9 Just past the bridge over Salmon Brook, turn left onto Granville Road (MA 189).

Tobacco barns are a common sight in the Connecticut River Valley.

5.3 At the blinking yellow light in North Granby, turn left onto East Street.

6.5 At the stop sign, turn left onto Vining Hill Road.
This rural road will take you into the area of the Jog.

8.9 At the stop sign, turn right onto Vining Hill Road.

9.9 At the light, cross US 202 and continue straight; the road is now MA 168.
There is a cluster of plazas in this busy area that has a few convenience stores and restaurants.

11.2 Pass between the Congamond Lakes.
Flat and wide tobacco fields dotted with long barns line the roads.

13.3 Continue on MA 168 as it turns sharply right.
One of the ride's bigger climbs will begin on this section.

15.6 At the blinking traffic light, turn left onto North Stone Road.
This road is much more rural and lightly traveled.

18.7 At a grassy triangle flanked by stop signs on either side, bear left onto Rising Corner Road.

18.9 At the stop sign, turn right onto South Longyard Road.
This residential area was once farmland; evident by the occasional field tucked among the housing developments.

21.8 At the stop sign, bear left onto Depot Street.

22.3 At the traffic light in Southwick, cross US 202 onto MA 57.
There are several stores in town if supplies are needed.

28.6 The ride ends at the village green in Granville.

Bicycle Shops

Custom Cycle, 88 Elm Street, Westfield; 413-568-6036

New Horizons Sports Inc., 55 Franklin Street, Westfield; 413-562-5237

Valley Bicycle & Repair Shop, Inc., 10 Hartford Avenue (CT 189), Granby, CT; 860-653-6545

27

The Connecticut River: Northampton to Sunderland

- ■ **DISTANCE:** 23.8 miles
- ■ **TERRAIN:** Mostly level terrain
- ■ **DIFFICULTY:** Easy
- ■ **RECOMMENDED BICYCLE:** Touring/road bike

This is one of the flattest routes in the book. Most of the ride follows the twisting course of the Connecticut River, through Northampton and Hatfield west of the river, and Sunderland and Hadley on the eastern riverbank. The roads are flanked by wide farm fields and pastures dotted with long wooden tobacco barns. Much of this area is protected by the Connecticut River Greenway State Park, 4,000 acres spread along 138 miles of the river.

The river flows more than 400 miles from the Canadian border to Long Island Sound in southern Connecticut, passing through fertile lowlands dotted with fields, barns, silos, and tobacco sheds. It's a pleasant area to ride in, popular among local cyclists.

The river is home to abundant wildlife; in the early morning and at dusk, there is a good chance you might glimpse a great blue heron along the riverbank, eyeing the water for frogs or fish. Hawks also soar above the river, as well as ospreys and the occasional American bald eagle.

Two features stand in stark contrast with this bucolic landscape: the commercial strip of US 5/MA 10 that joins the route for a short time, and the massive hulk of Mount Sugarloaf rising abruptly

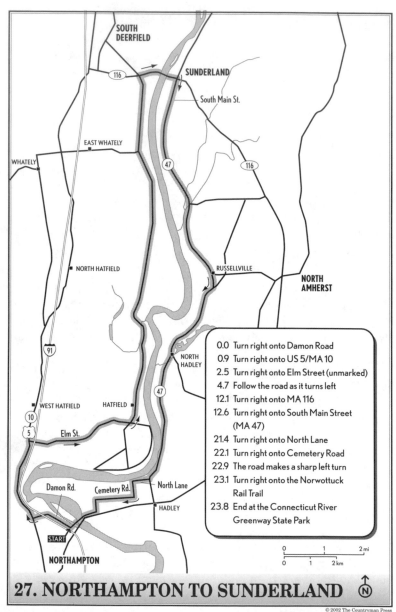

SOUTH
DEERFIELD

SUNDERLAND

116

South Main St.

EAST WHATELY

WHATELY

47

116

NORTH HATFIELD

RUSSELLVILLE

NORTH
AMHERST

91

NORTH
HADLEY

WEST HATFIELD   HATFIELD

47

10
5

Elm St.

Damon Rd.   Cemetery Rd.   North Lane

HADLEY

START

NORTHAMPTON

0.0	Turn right onto Damon Road
0.9	Turn right onto US 5/MA 10
2.5	Turn right onto Elm Street (unmarked)
4.7	Follow the road as it turns left
12.1	Turn right onto MA 116
12.6	Turn right onto South Main Street (MA 47)
21.4	Turn right onto North Lane
22.1	Turn right onto Cemetery Road
22.9	The road makes a sharp left turn
23.1	Turn right onto the Norwottuck Rail Trail
23.8	End at the Connecticut River Greenway State Park

0   1   2 mi
0   1   2 km

27. NORTHAMPTON TO SUNDERLAND

N

© 2002 The Countryman Press

from the valley floor north of Hatfield. This mountain of red sandstone, named for its resemblance to old-fashioned loaves of sugar, has a road to a summit observation tower. The reward for this lung-searing climb—a challenging option—are the stunning views into the river valley. King Philip used this strategic vantage point to survey Old Deerfield in 1675 before the Bloody Brook Massacre, the first of many brutal attacks on the historic farming village.

You'll return to Northampton on a bike path that crosses the Connecticut River on an abandoned railroad bridge at the western end of the old Boston & Maine Railroad line. The Norwottuck Rail Trail—named for the original 17th-century farming settlement that is now Hadley—also goes 8.5 miles east to Amherst. Another option for cycling in Northampton is the Northampton Bikepath, which starts downtown and heads 2.6 miles west to Look Memorial Park in Florence.

DIRECTIONS FOR THE RIDE

The ride begins at the Connecticut River Greenway State Park on Damon Road. There are several convenience stores in the Northampton area, as well as along the route in Hatfield, Sunderland, and Hadley.

0.0 Turn right out of the parking lot onto Damon Road.

0.9 At the traffic light, turn right onto US 5/MA 10.
Use caution on this heavily traveled road; watch for traffic entering and exiting shopping plazas.

2.5 Just before the I-91 entrance ramp, turn right onto Elm Street (unmarked), following the green sign for Hatfield.
Just after crossing the interstate, you'll be in rural farmland connected by small neighborhoods.

4.7 Follow the road as it curves left.
This is the center of Hatfield; notice the handsome antique homes lining Main Street. Tobacco and cornfields stretch out in either direction immediately upon leaving the village.

12.1 At the stop sign, turn right onto MA 116.
You will immediately cross the Connecticut River into the town of Sunderland. Nearby is the entrance to the Mount Sugarloaf State Reservation.

Mount Sugarloaf looms above the Connecticut River in Deerfield.

12.6 At the traffic light in Sunderland, turn right onto South Main Street (MA 47).
This side of the river is also relatively flat, with a few more rolling hills than the western side. When riding here in early spring, look for the telltale aluminum sap buckets hanging on maple trees along the road near the North Hadley Sugar Shack. Farther down the road, the Porter-Phelps-Huntington Historic House Museum is an 18th-century farm on the banks of the Connecticut River.

21.4 Turn right onto North Lane.

22.1 Turn right onto Cemetery Road.

22.9 Follow the paved road as it makes a sharp left turn (there will be a dirt road straight ahead).

23.1 Just before the stop sign, turn right onto the Norwottuck Rail Trail.
The bike path will take you back to Northampton on its own bridge over the Connecticut River.

23.8 The ride ends at the Connecticut River Greenway State Park.

Bicycle Shops

Autobike Inc., 16 Armory Street, Northampton; 413-585-1188
Northampton Bicycle, 319 Pleasant Street, Northampton; 413-586-3810
Peloton of Northampton, 15 State Street, Northampton; 413-584-1016

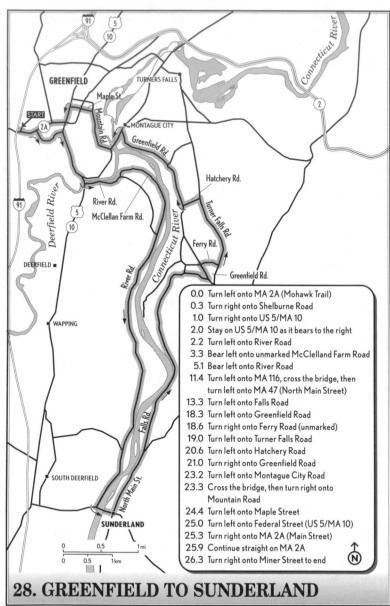

0.0 Turn left onto MA 2A (Mohawk Trail)
0.3 Turn right onto Shelburne Road
1.0 Turn right onto US 5/MA 10
2.0 Stay on US 5/MA 10 as it bears to the right
2.2 Turn left onto River Road
3.3 Bear left onto unmarked McClelland Farm Road
5.1 Bear left onto River Road
11.4 Turn left onto MA 116, cross the bridge, then turn left onto MA 47 (North Main Street)
13.3 Turn left onto Falls Road
18.3 Turn left onto Greenfield Road
18.6 Turn right onto Ferry Road (unmarked)
19.0 Turn left onto Turner Falls Road
20.6 Turn left onto Hatchery Road
21.0 Turn right onto Greenfield Road
23.2 Turn left onto Montague City Road
23.3 Cross the bridge, then turn right onto Mountain Road
24.4 Turn left onto Maple Street
25.0 Turn left onto Federal Street (US 5/MA 10)
25.3 Turn right onto MA 2A (Main Street)
25.9 Continue straight on MA 2A
26.3 Turn right onto Miner Street to end

28. GREENFIELD TO SUNDERLAND

The Connecticut River: Greenfield to Sunderland

- **DISTANCE:** 26.3 miles
- **TERRAIN:** Flat with several rolling hills; a 1.5-mile dirt road
- **DIFFICULTY:** Easy to moderate
- **RECOMMENDED BICYCLE:** Touring/road bike

This predominantly flat ride is a welcome respite from the hill country that surrounds it. The route follows the Connecticut River downstream from Greenfield, the commercial center of the upper Pioneer Valley and seat of Franklin County. Near Mount Sugarloaf it crosses the river and returns north through wide farmland on the opposite bank.

Greenfield was settled in 1686 by residents of nearby Deerfield who crossed the Green River and established a new community called the Green River District. The city is named for the fertile valley they farmed, which at the time was the northern frontier before the Canadian border. By the late 18th century, the settlement had cut its ties to Deerfield and began its transformation into a thriving mill town at the confluence of the Deerfield and Connecticut Rivers.

As you pedal through the bucolic farmland stretching along the Connecticut River, try to imagine Greenfield in the mid-1800s, when bustling riverfront mills produced cotton and wool, while others specialized in tanning hides and processing meat; there was also an iron foundry. The J. Russell Company built the nation's first cutlery factory on the river, producing half of America's supply of cutlery, including the famous Green River buffalo-skinning knife. One riverfront area was named Cheapside, after the 19th-century river port in London.

DIRECTIONS FOR THE RIDE
The ride begins at the Massachusetts Visitors Center behind the Howard Johnson restaurant on Miner Street, off MA 2A in Greenfield.

0.0 At the entrance to the visitors center, turn left onto MA 2A (Mohawk Trail). *Use caution in this busy, heavily congested area.*

0.3 At the second traffic light, turn right onto Shelburne Road, following the sign for US 5/MA 10 south. *Pass under a railroad trestle and through a quiet area of homes and small industry.*

0.8 Cross the Green River.

1.0 At the traffic light, turn right onto US 5/MA 10. Just past Meadows Golf Course, cross the Deerfield River.

2.0 Stay on US 5/MA 10 as it bears to the right, just before the bridge.

2.2 Past the bridge, turn left onto River Road. *After passing under the railroad trestle, this shady road becomes immediately quieter.*

3.3 Bear left onto unmarked McClelland Farm Road. (OPTION: Remain on River Road if you don't want to ride on a dirt road.) *This rural dirt road follows the river more closely than River Road and is seldom traveled.*

5.1 Bear left onto River Road. *The surroundings become very open, and the gently rolling road is flanked with farmland, tobacco barns, and cornfields. Along the way you'll pass the red barns of the University of Massachusetts Dairy Biotechnology Center, Agronomy Farm, and Turf Research Center.*

11.4 At the stop sign, turn left onto MA 116, immediately crossing the bridge over the Connecticut River into Sunderland. After the bridge, turn immediately left onto MA 47 (North Main Street).

It's hard to miss the massive sycamore tree growing along the road just past the bridge. A sign at the base of the tree left by the National Arborist Association claims that the tree was here in 1787 at the time of the signing of the U.S. Constitution. This avenue is full of Sunderland's oldest homes.

13.3 Turn left onto Falls Road at the sign for Blue Mountain Farm.

14.9 At the Montague town line, the road turns to Meadow Road.
The road eases closer to the river here and passes through flat farmland, offering several scenic views of the river.

18.3 At the T-intersection just after the bridge, turn left onto Greenfield Road.

18.6 Take the first right onto Ferry Road (unmarked).

19.0 At the stop sign, turn left onto Turner Falls Road.

20.6 Turn left onto Hatchery Road.
You'll pass the Bitzer State Fish Hatchery.

The Connecticut River flows slowly through the Pioneer Valley.

21.0 Turn right onto Greenfield Road.

23.2 At the stop sign, turn left onto Montague City Road.
Immediately cross the river here on a green metal bridge into the former Cheapside manufacturing district.

23.3 Cross the bridge at the Greenfield town line, then turn immediately right onto Mountain Road.
This steep 1-mile climb up Rocky Mountain is the biggest on the route. The Poet's Seat Tower at the summit commands a 360-degree view into the Connecticut River Valley. Greenfield resident and 19th-century poet Frederick Goddard Tuckerman often wrote while perched on the rocks where the western views inspired his nature writings. Tuckerman was a lesser-known contemporary of Ralph Waldo Emerson, Henry Wadsworth Longfellow, and Alfred, Lord Tennyson. The first tower built in 1879 was a smaller wooden structure; when it burned in 1911, the present three-story tower was built of native sandstone.

24.4 Turn left onto Maple Street.
This residential street will make you feel like you are back in town and the ride is nearing its end.

24.7 At the stop sign, go straight across Highland Avenue.
Use caution at this intersection; traffic from the left and right doesn't stop.

25.0 Turn left onto Federal Street (US 5/MA 10)

25.3 At the traffic light in the center of town, turn right onto MA 2A (Main Street), following signs toward Shelburne.
Use caution in this busy downtown area.

25.9 At the traffic light, continue straight on MA 2A.

26.3 At the Howard Johnson restaurant, turn right onto Miner Street to end the ride.

Bicycle Shops

Bicycle World, 104 Federal Street (US 5/MA 10), Greenfield; 413-774-3701
Bicycles Unlimited, 322 High Street, Greenfield; 413-772-2700

29

The Hamptons

- **DISTANCE:** 23.6 miles
- **TERRAIN:** Flat roads and low hills
- **DIFFICULTY:** Moderate
- **RECOMMENDED BICYCLE:** Touring/road bike

This ride introduces you to the Pioneer Valley's mix of farmland and brick mill towns. The area gets its name from the historic settlements along the 69-mile swath of Connecticut River lowlands that cuts through the state from north to south. Rolling and gentle hills flank the flat bottomland, and Mount Tom and Mount Holyoke rise precipitously from the valley floor. These two peaks form the backdrop for part of this ride.

Settlement and trade in the Pioneer Valley centered on the Connecticut River; in the 1800s it was heavily used for transportation and industry. During the Industrial Revolution, waterpower was harnessed to fuel the factories and mills that sprung up in towns along the river.

The ride begins in Northampton, the largest of the Hamptons on the tour. Locals call it NoHo, and it's also known as Paradise City, a name that dates back to the mid-19th century, when a mineral water spa drew travelers from around the world, including Swedish singer Jenny Lind, who called Northampton the Paradise of America.

Northampton has been an industrial and educational center

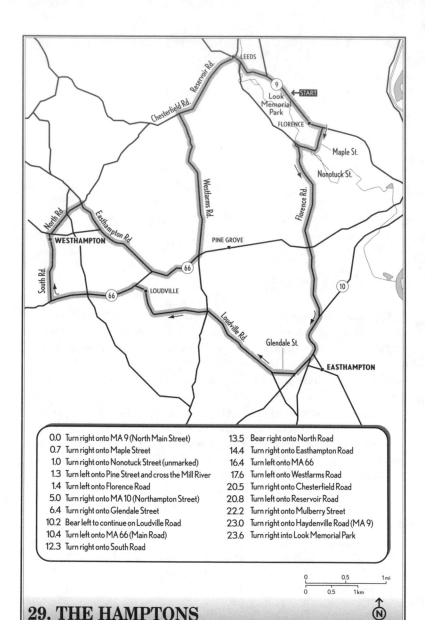

0.0	Turn right onto MA 9 (North Main Street)
0.7	Turn right onto Maple Street
1.0	Turn right onto Nonotuck Street (unmarked)
1.3	Turn left onto Pine Street and cross the Mill River
1.4	Turn left onto Florence Road
5.0	Turn right onto MA 10 (Northampton Street)
6.4	Turn right onto Glendale Street
10.2	Bear left to continue on Loudville Road
10.4	Turn left onto MA 66 (Main Road)
12.3	Turn right onto South Road
13.5	Bear right onto North Road
14.4	Turn right onto Easthampton Road
16.4	Turn left onto MA 66
17.6	Turn left onto Westfarms Road
20.5	Turn right onto Chesterfield Road
20.8	Turn left onto Reservoir Road
22.2	Turn right onto Mulberry Street
23.0	Turn right onto Haydenville Road (MA 9)
23.6	Turn right into Look Memorial Park

29. THE HAMPTONS

along the river since it was settled in 1654 and later became the seat of Hampshire County. The nation's 30th president, Calvin Coolidge, first practiced law here and served as the city's mayor. Resident Sylvester Graham was a leading advocate of vegetarianism and healthy eating but is immortalized for inventing a cracker and naming it after himself. The fiery minister Jonathan Edwards preached here for 23 years, until he moved on to Stockbridge in 1750. Smith College was founded here in 1875 for the "education of the intelligent gentlewoman"; the 125-acre campus of Gothic Revival buildings is surrounded by vibrant downtown streets crammed with nearly 100 shops and galleries and 75 restaurants.

It's an amazing concentration of culture given Northampton's rural location and small size. The outskirts are still overwhelmingly agricultural. You will pedal the back roads of Easthampton, Southampton, and Westhampton, which are lined with produce stands, farms, crop fields, and sugarhouses.

Easthampton sits near the Holyoke Range, whose peaks rise above the small town of stately old buildings as you head south from Northampton. Mount Tom State Reservation encompasses 1,800 wooded acres, and Arcadia Wildlife Sanctuary is a popular birding center that protects another 500 acres of woodland, fields, and marsh.

Westhampton is a classic New England farming village with a white clapboard Congregational Church and town hall on its tiny common. Its back roads climb hillsides, then run along open ridges with long views of hilltop farmland.

An abandoned railbed linking Northampton with Amherst across the Connecticut River is now a popular 10-mile bike path, an alternative for cyclists looking for a flat, easy ride. You can pick up the Northampton Bike Path at Look Memorial Park, follow it east for 2.6 miles to Elwell Recreation Area on the Connecticut River in Northampton, cross the river at the beginning of the Norwottuck Rail Trail, and follow it to Amherst along the old Boston & Maine Railroad line.

DIRECTIONS FOR THE RIDE

The ride begins in Look Memorial Park, a 200-acre oasis in Florence, donated by one of the city's great 19th-century industrialists. The park sits just west of downtown Northampton on MA 9.

0.0 At the park entrance, turn right onto MA 9 (North Main Street).
Use caution in busy downtown Florence.

0.7 At the traffic light, turn right onto Maple Street.

1.0 At the stop sign, turn right onto Nonotuck Street (unmarked).

1.3 At the stop sign, turn left onto Pine Street and cross the Mill River.

1.4 At the stop sign, turn left onto Florence Road.
This back road winds through a quiet residential neighborhood and becomes more rural as you head toward Easthampton.

3.7 At the traffic light, cross MA 66 and continue straight on Florence Road.

The Pioneer Valley abounds in pastoral scenes.

5.0 At the traffic light, turn right onto MA 10 (Northampton Street).
The village green in Easthampton is surrounded by handsome brick architecture and soaring church spires.

6.4 Turn right onto Glendale Street, following the sign for Westhampton.

7.3 At the blinking traffic light, continue straight onto Loudville Road.

10.2 Just past the falls, bear left at the unmarked Y-intersection to continue on Loudville Road.

10.4 At the stop sign, turn left onto MA 66 (Main Road).
Produce stands and orchards line this high road through rolling farmland.

12.3 Turn right onto South Road.

13.5 In the village of Westhampton, bear right at the Congregational Church onto North Road, following the sign for Williamsburg and Chesterfield.
A green shuttered Congregational Church and white clapboard town hall are among the handful of 18th-century buildings on the tiny green, which is surrounded by panoramic views of the distant hills.

14.1 Continue straight at the four-way intersection.

14.4 Turn right onto Easthampton Road, following the sign for Easthampton.

16.4 At the stop sign, turn left onto MA 66.

17.6 Turn left onto Westfarms Road.

18.3 Pass through the agricultural village of Westfarms.
There is a variety store along the road if you need supplies. The road soon leaves farmland and twists through woods, passing several sugarhouses along the way.

20.5 At the stop sign, turn right onto Chesterfield Road.

20.8 Turn left onto Reservoir Road.
A towering pine forest stretches along Roberts Meadow Reservoir. Much of this forest is a protected conservation area.

22.2 At the stop sign, turn right onto Mulberry Street, passing through the town of Leeds.

23.0 At the stop sign, turn right onto Haydenville Road (MA 9).

23.6 Turn right into Look Memorial Park in Florence to end the ride.

Bicycle Shops

Autobike Inc., 16 Armory Street, Northampton; 413-585-1188
Northampton Bicycle, 319 Pleasant Street, Northampton; 413-586-3810
Peloton of Northampton, 15 State Street, Northampton; 413-584-1016

30

Northampton to Chesterfield

- **DISTANCE:** 25.0 miles
- **TERRAIN:** Low hills with a couple steep climbs
- **DIFFICULTY:** Moderate to strenuous
- **RECOMMENDED BICYCLE:** Touring/road bike

This ride begins in Northampton and passes through flat Connecticut River lowlands, the kind of near-effortless riding typical of the Pioneer Valley. The route then explores the quiet Colonial villages of Chesterfield and Williamsburg on the eastern edge of the state's Hampshire Hills tourism region.

Northampton has had a colorful history since it was settled in 1654. Jonathan Edwards preached his fiery sermons here in the 18th century. Food pioneer and resident Sylvester Graham earned fame by inventing the graham cracker; his Pleasant Street home is now a restaurant and bakery. Calvin Coolidge was mayor of Northampton in the 1920s before rising to the presidency.

Silk manufacturing formed the backbone of Northampton's economy in the 19th century and employed more workers than any industry. Mulberry trees were planted to raise silk worms; textile mills then wove silk into goods, particularly thread. The industry declined in the early part of the 20th century, closing factories one by one in Northampton and throughout New England.

Thanks to a large community of artists, musicians, and craftspeople, the streets of Northampton are crammed with ethnic

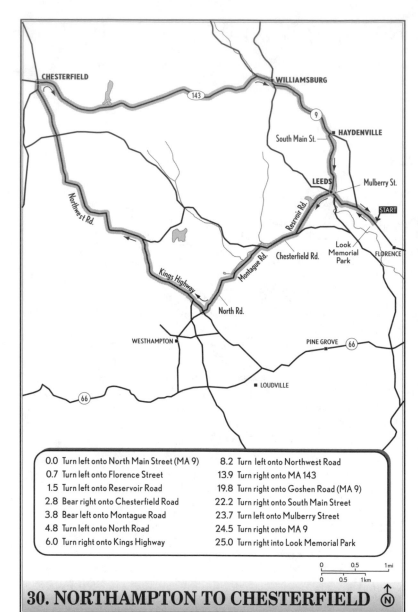

CHESTERFIELD

WILLIAMSBURG

143

9

South Main St.

HAYDENVILLE

LEEDS

Mulberry St.

Reservoir Rd.

START

Northwest Rd.

Chesterfield Rd.

Look
Memorial
Park

FLORENCE

Kings Highway

Montague Rd.

North Rd.

WESTHAMPTON

PINE GROVE

66

LOUDVILLE

66

0.0 Turn left onto North Main Street (MA 9)	8.2 Turn left onto Northwest Road
0.7 Turn left onto Florence Street	13.9 Turn right onto MA 143
1.5 Turn left onto Reservoir Road	19.8 Turn right onto Goshen Road (MA 9)
2.8 Bear right onto Chesterfield Road	22.2 Turn right onto South Main Street
3.8 Bear left onto Montague Road	23.7 Turn left onto Mulberry Street
4.8 Turn left onto North Road	24.5 Turn right onto MA 9
6.0 Turn right onto Kings Highway	25.0 Turn right into Look Memorial Park

0	0.5	1mi
0	0.5	1km

30. NORTHAMPTON TO CHESTERFIELD

N

restaurants, shops, galleries, and theaters. This eclectic, rather cosmopolitan small city has fewer than 30,000 residents but boasts the cultural offerings typical of much larger cities, earning the number one ranking in John Villani's book *Best Small Art Towns in America.*

This thriving arts scene is due in part to Northampton being home to Smith College, one of nine private colleges in the region and the largest private liberal arts college for women in the country.

The route begins in the Florence section of Northampton, known for its 19th-century silk mills and for Sojourner Truth, the freed slave-turned-abolitionist who lived here in the mid-1800s. Today it draws visitors to Look Memorial Park and its small zoo, swimming pools, and outdoor theater. The Miss Florence Diner has been a Main Street icon since the 1940s. Loyal patrons of this classic diner know it as Miss Flo's.

A couple of challenging climbs lead to the village of Chesterfield, a cluster of handsome white clapboard buildings on a lofty hilltop surrounded by rural farmland. The historic buildings include the 1848 town hall, Edward Memorial Museum, and 1835 Congregational Church, as well as the Bisbee Mill Museum, housed in a 19th-century gristmill.

Many of Williamsburg's 19th-century mills along the Mill River were destroyed in a devastating 1874 flood, but well-preserved historic buildings remain, including the Williamsburg General Store and the 1841 town hall. In the early 1800s, most residents lived in the steep hills of the Petticoat Hill Reservation, which you ride past before descending into the village. Its 60 acres of forest are dotted with hidden cellar holes and stone walls. Hiking trails to the top offer views of the village and the Connecticut River Valley, the Mill River, and the Holyoke Range.

Another option for cycling is the Norwottuck Rail Trail, a 10-mile paved bike path along MA 9 from Northampton to Amherst. From its start at the Connecticut Greenway State Park on Damon Road, it crosses the Connecticut River on an old railroad bridge, then passes through farms, woods, and marsh along the railbed once used by the Boston & Maine Railroad. Cyclists can also take the 2.6-mile Northampton Bike Path from downtown Northampton to Look Memorial Park in Florence.

DIRECTIONS FOR THE RIDE
The ride begins at Look Memorial Park on MA 9 in Florence, just west of downtown Northampton.

0.0 From the park entrance, turn left onto North Main Street (MA 9).

0.7 Turn left onto Florence Street, following the sign for Leeds.

1.5 At the post office in Leeds, turn left onto Reservoir Road.
This quiet, beautiful stretch of road follows the lakeshore and passes through a shady pine forest.

2.8 Bear right onto Chesterfield Road.

The Academy of Music is among the many architectural gems in downtown Northampton.

3.8 Bear left onto Montague Road.
This road winds through the woods as it leads into Westhampton, then opens to meadows and farm fields that follow a long ridge.

4.8 At the stop sign, turn left onto North Road.

6.0 At the stop sign, turn right onto Kings Highway.
This road immediately narrows, passes a farm, and climbs steeply toward Chesterfield.

8.2 At the four-way intersection, turn left onto Northwest Road.
This rolling, twisting rural road eventually reaches upland farms.

13.9 At the stop sign in the hilltop village of Chesterfield, turn right onto MA 143.
For the next 6 miles, this road descends toward Williamsburg.

19.8 At the stop sign, turn right onto Goshen Road (MA 9).
Among Williamsburg's Colonial buildings are shops, cafés, and a general store.

22.2 A sprawling brick factory building marks the village of Haydenville; turn right onto South Main Street, passing in front of the tiny yellow library.

22.8 At the Northampton town line, the road name changes to River Road.

23.7 At the stop sign, turn left onto Mulberry Street, which becomes Florence Street in Leeds.

24.5 At the stop sign, turn right onto MA 9.

25.0 Turn right into Look Memorial Park in Florence to end the ride.

Bicycle Shops

Autobike Inc., 16 Armory Street, Northampton; 413-585-1188
Northampton Bicycle, 319 Pleasant Street, Northampton; 413-586-3810
Peloton of Northampton, 15 State Street, Northampton; 413-584-1016

Let Backcountry Guides Take You There

Our experienced backcountry authors will lead you to the finest trails, parks, and back roads in the following areas:

50 Hikes Series
50 Hikes in the Adirondacks
50 Hikes in Colorado
50 Hikes in Connecticut
50 Hikes in Central Florida
50 Hikes in North Florida
50 Hikes in the Lower Hudson Valley
50 Hikes in Kentucky
50 Hikes in the Maine Mountains
50 Hikes in Coastal and Southern Maine
50 Hikes in Massachusetts
50 Hikes in Maryland
50 Hikes in Michigan
50 Hikes in the White Mountains
50 More Hikes in New Hampshire
50 Hikes in New Jersey
50 Hikes in Central New York
50 Hikes in Western New York
50 Hikes in the Mountains of North Carolina
50 Hikes in Ohio
50 More Hikes in Ohio
50 Hikes in Eastern Pennsylvania
50 Hikes in Central Pennsylvania
50 Hikes in Western Pennsylvania
50 Hikes in the Tennessee Mountains
50 Hikes in Vermont
50 Hikes in Northern Virginia
50 Hikes in Southern Virginia

Walking
Walks and Rambles on Cape Cod and the Islands
Walks and Rambles on the Delmarva Peninsula
Walks and Rambles in the Western Hudson Valley
Walks and Rambles on Long Island
Walks and Rambles in Ohio's Western Reserve
Walks and Rambles in Rhode Island
Walks and Rambles in and around St. Louis
Weekend Walks in St. Louis and Beyond
Weekend Walks Along the New England Coast
Weekend Walks in Historic New England

Bicycling
25 Bicycle Tours in the Adirondacks
25 Bicycle Tours on Delmarva
25 Bicycle Tours in Savannah and the Carolina Low Country
25 Bicycle Tours in Maine
25 Bicycle Tours in Maryland
25 Bicycle Tours in the Twin Cities and Southeastern Minnesota
30 Bicycle Tours in New Jersey
30 Bicycle Tours in the Finger Lakes Region
25 Bicycle Tours in the Hudson Valley
25 Bicycle Tours in Maryland
25 Bicycle Tours in Ohio's Western Reserve
25 Bicycle Tours in the Texas Hill Country and West Texas
25 Bicycle Tours in Vermont
25 Bicycle Tours in and around Washington, D.C.
25 Mountain Bike Tours in the Adirondacks
25 Mountain Bike Tours in the Hudson Valley
25 Mountain Bike Tours in Massachusetts
25 Mountain Bike Tours in New Jersey
Backroad Bicycling in Connecticut
Backroad Bicycling on Cape Cod, Martha's Vineyard, and Nantucket
Backroad Bicycling in Western Massachusetts
Backroad Bicycling in Eastern Pennsylvania
Backroad Bicycling in Wisconsin
The Mountain Biker's Guide to Ski Resorts
Bicycling America's National Parks: Arizona & New Mexico
Bicycling America's National Parks: California
Bicycling America's National Parks: Oregon & Washington
Bicycling America's National Parks: The Northern Rockies & Great Plains
Bicycling America's National Parks: Utah & Colorado
Bicycling Cuba

We offer many more books on hiking, fly-fishing, travel, nature, and other subjects. Our books are available at bookstores and outdoor stores everywhere. For more information or a free catalog, please call 1-800-245-4151 or write to us at The Countryman Press, P.O. Box 748, Woodstock, Vermont 05091. You can find us on the Internet at www.countrymanpress.com.